# THE UNCANNINESS OF UNSPEAKABLE ANXIETIES IN WEIRD FICTION

Daniel Nyikos

# THE UNCANNINESS OF UNSPEAKABLE ANXIETIES IN WEIRD FICTION

Daniel Nyikos

# TABLE OF CONTENTS

# INTRODUCTION

When we look to the places that frighten us, often we find uncomfortable truths about ourselves among the misshapen creatures and half-forgotten buildings on the fringes of the world we think we know. These are the spaces in which we are prepared to meet the liminal, the unsettling, and the repressed. Thus, weird fiction expresses contemporary social anxieties in a fascinating way, using these fears as a mechanism for driving plots of menace and horror. In such stories, tensions of race, sex, and class threaten the dominant hegemony with destabilization. While these stories grapple with these ambiguities and crossed boundaries, they do not all present change from the status quo in a positive way. While they sometimes challenge contemporary ideology, that system being undermined is often represented as proper and good, and the source of fear threatens the personal safety and/or sanity of those exposed to it. These texts also leave other assumptions unquestioned, instead reaffirming them. As such, the weird tale provides a fruitful and unique insight into the way these ideological problems were engaged with in fiction, at once exposing, challenging, and at times bolstering societal inequality and oppression.

While the weird story has a long tradition that continues vibrantly today, the form it took in the 1920s to the 1940s is at the center of my interest. As has been written about extensively, the early 20th century, when the weird tale came into its own, was a time of fundamental sociocultural change, and the weird story engaged with the anxieties, challenges, and opportunities created by this newness just as much as its cousins, the modernist stories in the slick literary magazines. The pulp designation these stories have been given is misleading. They delve into deeper and more disturbing places, and the possibilities they glimpse linger in the reader.

A modern reader might question the benefit of reexamining stories written almost century or more ago, particularly when it comes to contemporary cultural tensions such as xenophobia and the threat to perceived white exceptionalism and hegemony. A historicist reading would posit that these texts—and their authors—were products of their time, and that as such they reproduced contemporary biases. We imagine that we have progressed past this point. We participate in a rich postcolonial and feminist discourse that did not exist in the first half of the 20th century; we challenge the problematic elements of our own culture and thinking and seek more inclusive narratives. It is easy to fall into the trap of imagining that we live in a different, more enlightened age, but this distances us from these ideologies and positions us in a place of complacency. As we look at these texts, we see that they explicitly engage with racist, misogynistic, and other ideologies of power. Weird fiction often includes appeals against hegemonic systems of representation, such as Ignosi's speech about the greed and destruction caused by colonialism in King Solomon's Mines or the undermining of hypermasculine patriarchy in the Northwest Smith stories. What we find when we examine these texts is that, even while they question some ideas, they accept others uncritically, reproducing damaging narratives at the same time as they challenge others. By critically reading these texts, we gain insight into our own ways of shaping and transmitting complex ideologies, and we also challenge how we imagine our own relationship with these ideas.

Scholarship about weird fiction, while expanding, remains sparse, partly due to the academic bias against what is perceived as popular, lower-class art. I first came to the writings of Robert E. Howard in grade school and those of H. P. Lovecraft in high school. Both were formative experiences. They opened new worlds to me, worlds that changed my own. The thing that drew me most to the writings of these authors, as well as to others writing in the weird tale tradition, is the way they combine the weird with the real. They not only unfold new vistas of untold worlds, they make the world around us weird. To borrow Shklovsky's term, they defamiliarize my surroundings, leading me back to my own familiar streets with the same wide-eyed wonder and perhaps even trepidation I felt accompanying the protagonists of their stories. They dare to explore open-eyed the things that disturb them. Those who dismiss the genre's potential out of the belief that no profound idea could emerge from stories of tentacled behemoths or strange sorcery forget, perhaps, that the tradition of telling our own stories with weird elements stretches back at least as far as Homer.

Weird fiction creates, by its nature, a relationship with contemporary culture, desires, and fears that lie at the heart of its creation. The tensions that a member of society usually represses in order to function within the ideological bounds of their social sphere are expressed and explored through this medium. This mirrors Freud's model of the return of the uncanny, an effect key to weird fiction. As Freud explains in a much-quoted passage from his seminal essay The Uncanny, the uncanny effect can be created by "the actual repression of a particular content and a return of what has been repressed."[1] By this function, the employment of the uncanny in literature is essentially linked to revealing repressed cultural tensions.

This is Freud's second defined source for the uncanny, the first being a moment of doubt about whether ghosts and other supernatural forces, which the modern mind has dismissed, might exist after all. This first definition

---

[1] Sigmund Freud, *The Uncanny.* Trans. David McLintock, London: Penguin Books, 2003, 155.

certainly covers much of what we see in weird literature, but, as Freud points out about the uncanny in literature, "it embraces the whole of this and something else besides,"[2] revealing that in literature the uncanny exists in both forms simultaneously: as the supernatural and as repressed fears.

The first effect is clear in weird fiction: the horror of a Lovecraftian shoggoth—whose existence the rational modern mind rejects—summons up repressed childhood fears of monsters, darkness, and the unknown. But this is not the only repressed fear lurking in the subconscious—nor, for that matter, is this the only fear the shoggoth represents. Vivian Ralickas explains, "the soft, plastic, amorphous, anarchistic, innately perverse, and infinitely adaptable Shoggoths encapsulate a form of radical, inassimilable alterity that poses a threat to any ordered civilization."[3] Through monsters, Lovecraft expressed his fear of the downfall of white civilization and the toppling of white Anglo men as the dominant power in the world.

As this example shows, the uncanny is born of societal pressures, as the repressions that ideologies require are challenged and subverted. We can find examples of this throughout weird literature, and I have explored them in this book: how race, class, and gender are all problematized through a subgenre that reproduces contemporary tensions through uncanny elements, using these to further defamiliarize norms and contend with what might otherwise be taboo or unchallenged beliefs.

The readers of Weird Tales were used to tales of the unexpected in which expectations were subverted: this could be just as true for race, class, and gender as it was for contemporary and traditional narrative structure. Beyond the surprise of crossing the uncanny border into revealing the existence of monsters and worlds beyond the known, weird fiction crosses other borders of repressed cultural issues and conflicts.

The writers of these stories are positioned to reflect critically on contemporary society. They are almost always outsiders, shut out of literary and academic respectability by their preferred story, an exclusion they often reverse by depicting themselves as uniquely imaginative and sensitive to ideas their contemporaries cannot understand. These visions sweep the reader into an exciting place of destabilization and possibility. They even anticipate philosophical and theoretical advancements that came decades later. We can find Julia Kristeva's abjection in the unnamable horrors of Lovecraft's stories, or even the philosophy of life and biopolitics in the figure of Howard's Conan the Cimmerian. These stories erupted from a turbulent social era. They are immersed in a bold uniqueness that enables them to explore ideas that others would shrink from. Thus, the weird tales present a

---

[2] Ibid., 155.

[3] Vivian Ralickas, "'Cosmic Horror' and the Question of the Sublime in Lovecraft," *Journal of the Fantastic in the Arts* 18 no. 3 (2007): 380, accessed March 30, 2017, http://www.jstor.org/stable/24351008.

fertile garden for philosophical inquiry.

The aim of this book is to contribute meaningful literary analysis to the scholarship available about the magazine Weird Tales in particular and about weird fiction as a sub-genre in general. As a search of a university article database will readily show, there are sadly few sources easily accessible for scholars to use. This is especially unfortunate because in the last few decades there has been such a commendable amount of attention paid to the writers of Weird Tales, particularly Lovecraft and Howard. Sadly, even when these studies are peer reviewed, such as in The Dark Man: The Journal of Robert E. Howard Studies, they are not made available through online databases, leaving valuable scholarly work inaccessible to the majority of those who would read it and use it as a basis of entering into the conversation about weird literature. It is particularly important to make literary criticism of weird fiction available to undergraduate students and others who are starting to become interested in the subject, as more accessible research material will not only expand their understanding of the topic as a scholarly discourse but also support their own forays into writing about the field.

I have chosen to focus my methods on close readings of weird fiction, treating it as a valuable literary expression and searching for deep meanings, contradictions, and explorations of contemporary anxieties. The interwar period, which saw the flowering and deaths of H. P. Lovecraft and Robert E. Howard, saw sociocultural shifts that the weird fiction of the time grapples with. Before the First World War, the idealistic dreams of the Victorian era and its wholehearted belief in progress and respectability had already been cracked by fin de siècle artistic circles including the Decadents and increasing voices of discontent about American and European colonialisms. Millions starved in British India under decades of drought, and the bloody colonial wars for Africa were condemned by voices such as Joseph Conrad's. The rapid progress of technology and its promise of less work and more time dedicated to the ennobling of the soul died in the trenches of the First World War as the economic engines of the world turned themselves to destruction on an industrial scale, churning out poison gas, barbed war, and artillery. After the war, many women pressed for equality and sexual liberation, and the vibrant flapper became a symbol of the new, political, bold woman. Modernist writers like Gertrude Stein and Virginia Woolf, rejecting traditional narrative structures, turned their attention to the depths of the human mind, using stream-of-consciousness narrative to reveal doubts and complexities within the middle-class psyche that were previously repressed. With these in mind, I employ postcolonial, feminist, and psychoanalytical readings to examine weird fiction's conversation with the profound social pressures of its time.

Much of the available scholarship on Weird Tales examines it through a historicist lens, looking at the stories in its pages as a reflection of the era in which they were written. This perspective, for example, includes the ongoing debate about H. P. Lovecraft's xenophobia, in which a point of repeated contention is whether Lovecraft was especially racist "for his age." In other ways, the authors and stories of the magazine have also been examined as predecessors for modern work, tracing the development of modern literary themes: this backwards-looking perspective has focused on the elements that continue to influence literature and broader culture today. It is easy to find, for example, many texts from the last few decades shaped by Lovecraft's unnamable horrors or Howard's brooding warriors and menacing sorcerers. As the New Historicist critics remind us, this perspective skews our perspective by reading our own modern horizon of expectations onto the original texts, using the elements that have become popular as a basis of examination. Just as there is much that remains and is reinvented every few decades, there is much that has been forgotten about the weird tale. By reading them only as part of a longer continuity, we both do these texts a disservice and become complacent in our own ways of thinking.

At the Popular Culture Association/American Culture Association conferences I attended in San Antonio in 2011 and Boston in 2012, the weird fiction discussion was grouped under Pulp Studies, and much of the conversation about weird fiction takes place under those auspices. A review of the conference program for 2016 in Seattle shows that this continues to be the case.[4] Weird fiction has only some connections with its peers in pulp magazines such as Western or masked detective stories. Instead of looking at it chiefly as a pulp product, I see the weird tale as part of a longer and broader continuity in literature. It is my belief, therefore, that the most rewarding and accurate way of discussing weird tales is as part of a web of influence, adaptation, and inspiration that stretches back to the Gothic writers the weird story writers admired, not to mention poets and tale-tellers from the writers of Classical epics to medieval romances to tales of wonder from India and the Middle East. H. P. Lovecraft explicitly rejected contemporary modernist literature and sought out writers from the past he found more sympathetic, such as Edgar Allan Poe. While Robert E. Howard was influenced by writers of pulp historical fiction such as Harold Lamb and Talbot Mundy, he also read H. Rider Haggard and other Victorian adventure writers, whose perceptions of empire and the colonialist enterprise found their way into his own imagination.

In this collection, I examine the way the writers of Weird Tales magazine, especially the writers who corresponded closely with H. P. Lovecraft who became known as the Lovecraft Circle, actively engaged in a conversation with their multifaceted influences, including histories, biographies, poetry,

---

[4] Popular Culture Association/American Culture Association, "PCA/ACA Program with Schedule," accessed March 2, 2017, http://pcaaca.org/wp-content/uploads/2016/05/2016-pcaaca-program-with-schedule.pdf.

and various forms of early fantastic fiction. For this reason, I have included a number of essays about the texts that would influence the writers of Weird Tales, stories that—in many cases retroactively—became identified with weird literature. These texts, some of which are canonized texts of Victorian literature, have long been treated with the seriousness they deserve and examined closely for their textual richness. The close readings that these major works lend themselves to can also be rewardingly applied to later works of weird fiction. It is clear that the same complex explorations of themes that appear in their influences would later appear in the works of the Weird Tales writers who so admire these texts, and I explore the latter in terms of the same representative function we are used to seeing in the former. Throughout my readings, I explore ways the texts both challenge and unquestioningly affirm contemporary biases of sex/gender, class, and race.

Thus, I examine three of the major influences on the tradition of the weird tale dating from the Victorian era. First, I look at H. Rider Haggard's King Solomon's Mines and explore ways the text problematizes race and imperialism through the interaction of English men and African people and places. The text contains many unexamined representations of contemporary racial ideologies, including the white savior figure, but it also engages with them in other ways that create an ambiguous and self-critical work. In the second chapter, I reexamine The Strange Case of Dr. Jekyll and Mr. Hyde, arguing for the text's use of contemporary cultural anxieties related to hypocrisy and moral corruption to question the Jekyll/Hyde dichotomy and suggest that Hyde, in fact, is merely a vessel for Jekyll to engage in the behaviors he already desires but dares not for fear of public censure. In the third chapter, I pursue a similar reading of Arthur Machen's The Great God Pan, a huge influence on Lovecraft, demonstrating how, in addition to its famous cosmic horror elements, it stages problems of sex, class, and morality that it is uniquely positioned to suggest through its use of weird elements.

In the fourth chapter, I perform an overview of the Lovecraft Circle and their writing community. The writers, marked by outsiderness by their chosen medium and often by social factors, constructed their own argument for the superiority of their own aesthetics. The sensitivity that so often appears in their stories as a sign of a superior mind became the mark of their own claim to authority based in their alternative canon. While transgressive in their implicit argument about the validity of an alternative literary aesthetic and oeuvre, these writers continued to uphold oppressive beliefs about class, sex, and race.

The rest of the book studies these effects more closely in the individual work of Lovecraft and Howard. The fifth chapter examines Lovecraft's "Dreams in the Witch House" as a product of this weird effect, tracing the uncanny effect of the combination of folklore and mathematics as a parallel of the tension between the known and unknown, the experiences and the imagined in weird fiction. In the next chapter, I look specifically at how Julia Kristeva's theory of abjection illuminates the uncanny events of "The Colour Out of Space," in which an unsignifyable element arrives from beyond all that is known by human consciousness and literally disintegrates the world we think we know. Robert E. Howard's technique for incorporating research and other writers' work into his own texts while shaping both to his own aesthetic forms the basis of my sixth chapter. The eighth chapter finishes read Howard's Conan stories using the political philosophy of Giorgio Agamben, demonstrating how Conan's powerful combined identity of bandit and king aligns with the biopower theory of the homo sacer and the violence inherent in sovereign power.

These writers repeat some contemporary perspectives on popular themes and also problematize and grapple with others. They take advantage of a medium centered in possibilities and an audience primed to embrace the disturbing and new, using it to engage with problematic issues from gender to race to modernity, and they do so in ways that varies from story to story, as every story takes the form of a meditation and exploration on the varied matrix of reflections, experiences, and concerns of the author, shifting from moment to moment and from thought to thought. Some writers, such as Lovecraft, express repellant opinions in personal correspondence and in their stories. In his writing, he opens windows to self-doubt about the fears these opinions connect with. In some cases the conflicts these create find surprisingly complex expression in his work. For example, Lovecraft expresses his fears that, when seen through science and the immense depths of space and time, the differences between people of color and white people—a difference on which much of his personal esteem rested—disappears.

This does not excuse the often shockingly offensive ideologies these writers advance—in many cases challenged or even discredited at the time of their writing. An example of this can be found in the novel The Hour of the Dragon by Robert E. Howard, which employs the method of typing characters by their race found in many weird tales. Ethnic origin is deterministic in Howard's work: Conan's own legendary prowess is often attributed to his Cimmerian background. Thus, racial essentialism is represented as natural and hierarchical: given races are better at given things, including leadership. This ideology is derived partially from Theosophical works about "root races" and contemporary theories about eugenics, all of which helped reinforce notions of white racial superiority. This is particularly true in Howard's depictions of black characters.

In describing slaves freeing themselves and taking revenge on their oppressors, the novel creates an ideological contradiction: on the one hand, sympathy naturally lies with the oppressed, but on the other, the free will and equality of people of color is nevertheless suppressed by the narrative, which continues to depict them as inferior. When presenting the revolt of "Kushite" slaves against their white masters, the narrator describes the black men as though they were bestial and savage: "The blacks were frothing crazy now, shaking and tearing at their chains and shrieking the name of Amra like an invocation."[5] The terms explicitly compare them to demons and animals: "a blind, black torrent, screaming like fiends, smiting with broken oars and pieces of iron, tearing and rending with talons and teeth."[6] Thus, the black men, even when reclaiming their freedom from their captors—something Conan himself has just done in a heroic moment—are shown not as men reclaiming their subjecthood but as animals bursting from their pens.

As soon as the former slaves take over the ship, they are given subservient identities again by Conan, who takes them on as his crew even as he promises them better treatment, setting himself in the position of their former slavemasters, though a "better" one. It is easy to see in this scene a retelling of the paternalistic ideologies of the antebellum South, in which Conan plays the part of the benevolent white master who guides the slaves to a better life under his control. In an image born of white supremacist ideology, Conan is described as "the blood-stained giant about whom the chanting blacks thronged to cast themselves prostrate on the bloody deck and beat their heads against the boards in an ecstasy of hero-worship."[7] The former slaves are never described as individuals, nor do they play any part beyond following Conan's orders and acting lost with him gone. Thus, the narrative itself denies them subjecthood.

These deep-rooted issues cause us to look beyond these texts to think how such a history influences the works it has touched. Even as I present it in context, it is important to look beyond the 1940s, as the Weird Tales of the Lovecraft Circle did not represent an end point in the tradition of the weird story, but rather one venue for the publication of what is a very broad spectrum of storytelling that encompasses everything from historical romances to early science fiction. The weird tale as a sub-genre can easily be traced into the contemporary period in the writings of authors such as Stephen King and Gabriel Garcia Marquez, as well as in the magical realist works of writers such as Kelly Link and China Mieville. We must consider how many of the basic ideological constructs of the weird fiction genre, such as its reliance on the fear of the Other, continue to be reproduced. The influence of H. P. Lovecraft alone is so tremendous that is has provided fodder for countless bachelor's theses, and it would be a tedious and by-now redundant task to attempt a full exploration of the effect of his ideas on the modern literary scene.

It is enough to note that, while the boundaries of what constitutes weird

---

[5] Robert E. Howard, *The Bloody Crown of Conan,* New York: Ballantine Books.191
[6] Ibid., 192.
[7] Ibid., 192.

fiction have mostly dissolved, traces of it remain strong in disparate areas. In fact, we should remember that what actually defines a weird tale has always been ambiguous. Lovecraft's seminal essay "Supernatural Horror in Literature" features a definition by which many, if not most, of the stories in Weird Tales itself would not, in fact, qualify as weird tales. One must wonder whether Lovecraft had in mind any writer but himself when he wrote it:

> The true weird tale has something more than secret murder, bloody bones, or a sheeted form clanking chains according to rule. A certain atmosphere of breathless and unexplainable dread of outer, unknown forces must be present; and there must be a hint, expressed with a seriousness and portentousness becoming its subject, of that most terrible conception of the human brain—a malign and particular suspension or defeat of those fixed laws of Nature which are our only safeguard against the assaults of chaos and the daemons of unplumbed space.[8]

A more appropriate, though far more ambiguous, definition might be found in the subtitle of Weird Tales itself: "the unique magazine," whose stories simply could not have been published elsewhere. Here we see already the weird tale as an amalgamation, one which encompasses everything from the grotesque fantastic satires of Clark Ashton Smith to the supernatural detective stories of Seabury Quinn. Despite Lovecraft's insistence to the contrary, many of the stories in Weird Tales fall back on familiar tropes of ghosts, curses, vampires, and werewolves; in fact, some appear to have no supernatural element at all. The uniqueness, then, is universally one of perspective. The stories, like the writers who created them, approach their subjects from new angles. Like the unguessed angles described so often by Lovecraft, these might seem impossible to those of us used to the ideology of the familiar world, but their inclusion inevitably shakes us from that comfortable shell and introduces us to new possibilities—though we must always keep in mind what is being left unsaid and unchallenged, and thus reaffirmed.

It is these possibilities that form the most fascinating part of the weird tale's effect for me. Behind the bizarre backdrop we glimpse disturbing flashes of our world returned back to us, made strange. We see the hypocrisy of middle-class morality, the brutal inequality of the treatment of women and other races, deep fears of widespread societal change, and in every case the ability to enter into conversation about these issues with the imagination of those who, their minds trained by the weird, are able to imagine possibilities beyond the entrenched doctrines we know from our own world. Writers and readers of this subgenre must continue to actively and consciously question

---

[8] H. P. Lovecraft, "Supernatural Horror in Literature," *The H. P. Lovecraft Archive,* accessed on February 15, 2017, http://www.hplovecraft.com/writings/texts/essays/shil.aspx

the underlying assumptions left at the heart of these tales. As such, the weird story continues to be vital and relevant today, constantly reinventing itself to challenge an ever-changing world.

## Bibliography

Freud, Sigmund. *The Uncanny*. Trans. David McLintock, London: Penguin Books, 2003.

Howard, Robert E. *The Bloody Crown of Conan*. New York: Ballantine Books.

Lovecraft, H. P. "Supernatural Horror in Literature." *The H. P. Lovecraft Archive*. Accessed on February 15, 2017. http://www.hplovecraft.com/writings/texts/essays/shil.aspx

Popular Culture Association/American Culture Association. "PCA/ACA Program with Schedule." Accessed March 2, 2017. http://pcaaca.org/wp-content/uploads/2016/05/2016-pcaaca-program-with-schedule.pdf

Ralickas, Vivian. "'Cosmic Horror' and the Question of the Sublime in Lovecraft." *Journal of the Fantastic in the Arts* 18 no. 3 (2007): 364-398. Accessed March 30, 2017. http://www.jstor.org/stable/24351008.

# BOUNDARIES CROSSED AND UNCROSSED: RACE AND EMPIRE IN H. RIDER HAGGARD'S *KING SOLOMON'S MINES*

As I mentioned earlier, the aim of this collection is to explore the potential of weird fiction as a means of cultural critique and even subversion. In looking at the origins of the weird tale, we can also look beyond domestic stories to the imperialistic adventure tales that inspired many weird fiction writers, such as Robert E. Howard. Among Howard's influences were Sir Arthur Conan Doyle, Rudyard Kipling, Jack London, Harold Lamb, and Talbot Mundy. In a letter to H. P. Lovecraft, Howard listed H. Rider Haggard as one of "my favorite writers."[9] Rusty Burke lists three Haggard novels that we know Howard read or owned: *Allan Quatermain*, *The Ancient Allan*, and *People of the Mist*. In "The Ancient Allison," Charles R. Rutledge demonstrates a direct influence of Haggard on Howard in Howard's borrowing of a particular mystical plant that allows those who eat it to have visions of their past lives, a plot device in *The Ancient Allan*[10].

*King Solomon's Mines* is the first Allan Quatermain novel and among Haggard's most famous. As such, it offers valuable insight into the way race and empire were represented and problematized in Haggard's work. Despite its standard plot of white explorers traveling into "Darkest Africa" to pursue its untold riches, the novel proves on closer reading to be racially complex. It explicitly challenges many of the racist assumptions of contemporary race theory, but it also accepts many of the values underpinning these theories at face value, such as the inherent separation of races. Given the presence of these themes in the source material, it is then worthwhile to explore the question of similar themes in the weird fiction influenced by Haggard.

The writings of Haggard have been dismissed almost since they were published. Many critics dismiss his novels as shallow masculine adventure at best. C.S. Lewis "condemned him [Haggard] as insufferably shallow" and George Orwell "could barely bring himself to include *She* in a list of 'good

---

[9] Rusty Burke, "The Robert E. Howard Bookshelf," *REHupa*, accessed February 15, 2017, http://web.archive.org/web/20150201233852/http://www.rehupa.com/OLDWEB/bookshelf.htm

[10] Charles R. Rutledge, "The Ancient Allison," *Singular Points*, accessed February 15, 2017, http://singular--points.blogspot.hu/2011/01/ancient-allison.html

bad books"[11]. Yet these critics fail to account for the anti-imperialist, anti-racist, and anti-colonialist content of these works demonstrate by deconstructing such attitudes within the framework of a journey by Englishmen into unknown lands.

Published in 1885, Henry Rider Haggard's novel *King Solomon's Mines* is in many respects a prototypical Victorian adventure novel. It is frequently cited as the first example of the Dark Continent genre. From beginning to end, it tells of elephant hunts, perilous voyages into uncharted Africa, dark magic, pitched battles, fantastic wealth, weird rituals, remarkable coincidence, and the ultimate triumph of a small group of brave Englishmen faced with overwhelming odds. This novel is in many ways symptomatic of Victorian attitudes of racial superiority and the inherent inferiority of African cultures.

Many of Haggard's contemporaries rejected the possibility of an advanced African civilization. In an article in *History in Africa*, Daniel Tangri claims "Haggard believed that the local Bantu were too primitive to have produced anything so monumental [as the ancient city of the novel], and opted in favor of Mediterranean colonists"[12]. While the great Colossi and roads were, in the story, probably built by King Solomon, Phoenicians, or Egyptians—the characters never discover which—Haggard does not believe the locals are "too primitive" to build such things, but rather suggests they are wise enough not to, understanding the dangers of greed and foreign aggression that comes from wealth. Haggard's novel presents the civilization of the Kukuanas as equivalent to that of the English both in nobility and in military prowess. Throughout the novel, Haggard invites the reader to contrast the traditionally English opinions of Allan Quatermain, the narrator of the novel, with the alternatives suggested by the events of the novel. It is precisely because Quatermain fails so completely to account for the complexity of the events around him, even while unconsciously acknowledging them, that the novel sets up a thematic conflict between Quatermain's unquestioned racism and the events he experiences in Africa.

As noted, many scholars read Quatermain's narration as an uncomplicated presentation of Haggard's own racism and misogyny. In an article in *Victorian Literature and Culture*, Heidi Kaufman describes the three male protagonists symbolically raping not only a feminized Africa, but also

---

[11] Norman A. Etherington, "Rider Haggard, Imperialism, and the Layered Personality," *Victorian Studies*, 22, no. 1 (1978): 72, accessed February 15, 2017, http://www.jstor.org/stable/3826929.

[12] Daniel Tangri, "Popular Fiction and the Zimbabwe Controversy," *History in Africa* 17 (1990), 295, accessed February 15, 2017, http://search.ebscohost.com/login.aspx?direct=true&db=edsjsr&AN=edsjsr.10.2307.31718 18.

the figurative "passive male body" of King Solomon[13]. Although such readings doubtless explore complex issues at play in the novel, they fail to address how Haggard's text deconstructs these ideals. Rather than merely demonstrating and producing normative Victorian attitudes, the novel presents them through a narrator who obviously fails to grasp both the literal and symbolic significance of the events he experiences. Haggard thus invites the reader to pursue a more nuanced reading that his narrator, an old English elephant hunter set in his ways, cannot.

## Background

In 1885, the Zulu War was still fresh in the memory of the British public. The better-equipped British army suffered bloody early losses, shocking the English public. Before the war, it would have been thought preposterous for the British to face defeat at the hands of an African nation whose warriors were armed with spears in the face of modern European firepower. During the war, the young Haggard served in South Africa, and so would have had first-hand experience of both the arrogance of the English imperial powers and the shock to the established principles of racial superiority of such a defeat.

As Alexandra Fuller writes in her introduction to the 2002 The Modern Library edition, "Haggard would have been witness to the Zulus' defeat of the British on January 22, 1879, at Isandhlwana during the Zulu War.... Perhaps it was this experience that led to his understanding that the white-colonial-master-race attitude had a limited life, and a limited reality, in Africa"[14]. Fuller cites several examples of the racial complications of the novel, culminating in the love between the English Captain Good and the African Foulata. It is the task of this essay to go beyond Fuller's brief treatment of these examples in order to demonstrate in concrete terms the techniques Haggard uses to undermine—no pun intended—the colonialist and racial rhetoric which Quatermain subscribes to in the novel.

The Zulus are used extensively in the novel, and are spoken of in high terms. When their servant Umbopa, who later reveals himself to be Ignosi, the king of Kukuanaland, speaks poetically of his philosophy of life, Quatermain notes that such "strange bursts of rhetorical eloquence that the Zulus sometimes indulge in... show that the race is by no means devoid of poetic instinct and poetic power"[15]. It is worth pausing here to note the "strange" that Quatermain feels compelled to include, unable to accept

---

[13] Heidi Kaufman, "'King Solomon's Mines?:' African Jewry, British Imperialism, and H. Rider Haggard's Diamonds," *Victorian Literature and Culture* 33, no. 2 (2005): 518, accessed February 15, 2017, http://www.jstor.org/stable/25058726.

[14] Alexandra Fuller, introduction to *King Solomon's Mines* (New York: The Modern Library, 2002), xxiv.

[15] Henry Rider Haggard, *King Solomon's Mines* (New York: The Modern Library, 2002), 50.

without a marker of Otherness the equivalence between white and black poetry. To cement the connection between Ignosi and the mighty Zulu nation, we learn that Ignosi was present at the battle of Isandhlwana. We are also given a glimpse into Quatermain's later realization of his own racist thinking when he admits, "At the time I told him to hold his tongue, and leave such matters to wiser heads; but afterwards I thought of his words"[16]. This is not the first suggestion we get of Alan Quatermain's unreliability as a guide to the complex relationships of this novel, though he fails to completely grasp the damage of dismissing the opinions of an African—which proved wiser than those of the English. From the beginning, the Zulu War is presented as a model of the failure of British imperialism in Africa: because the British did not understand the threat the Zulus faced as an organized fighting force, they suffered greatly for it.

The Zulus are clearly an inspiration for the African nation of the novel. The natives in Kukuanaland constitute what might be Haggard's version of a perfected Zulu nation, being "much superior to that [country] inaugurated by Chaka in Zululand, inasmuch as permits of even more rapid mobilization, and does not necessitate the employment of the pernicious system of forced celibacy"[17]. The narrator, Quatermain, speaks with admiration of the "domestic and family customs of the Kukuanas" and of their "smelting and welding of metals"[18]. Rather than merely an African nation to be conquered, Kukuanaland is not only unspoiled by an imperialist aggressor but also able to resist colonization through strength of arms, as the Zulus successfully did for so long.

## Alan Quatermain as Unreliable Interpreter

Almost from the beginning, the novel invites the reader to draw different conclusions about the content of the novel than Quatermain does. When he is introducing the novel, the narrator seems to echo *David Copperfield*'s famous introduction when he says, "I wonder what sort of a history it will be when I have finished it, if I ever come to the end of the trip!"[19]. Quatermain at least claims to have no clear understanding of the events in mind that he wishes to convey, and as such leaves interpretation open to the reader.

The first pages stress Quatermain's unsuitability as a judge of the events by his early expressed interest in the "Ingoldsby Legends"[20], which the notes of the Modern Library edition identify as "clever and absurd prose stories and poems, most of which were based on medieval fables and legends"[21]. At

---

[16] Ibid., 34.
[17] Ibid., 4
[18] Ibid., 4.
[19] Ibid., 5.
[20] Ibid., 5.
[21] Ibid., 239.

the height of the climactic battle of the novel, Quatermain's mind becomes filled with "Warlike fragments from the 'Ingoldsby Legends'"[22]. These surely demonstrate Quatermain's absurdly European way of seeing his struggles through antiquated medieval notions. His own imperialist beliefs are no more relevant to the Africa of the novel than the medieval legends are to modern warfare.

We are also given a look into Quatermain's system of beliefs and the novel's deconstruction thereof when Quatermain speaks of the injury to his leg which pains him. When he writes, "It is a hard thing when one has shot sixty-five lions and more,… that the sixty-sixth should chew your leg like a quid of tobacco. It breaks the routine of the thing, and… I am an orderly man and don't like that"[23]. Already, the reader has an idea of Quatermain as a man set in his outdated notions who does not look beyond the "routine of the thing," and has suffered thereby. It is not difficult to see the reflection of this in his behavior toward the Africans in the novel.

This behavior can already be seen in his reaction to the bold language employed by Umbopa/Ignosi. When the young man dares to address them as "O white men" instead of "O Inkosis" [chiefs], Quatermain rebukes him: "You forget yourself a little…. Your words come out unawares. That is not the way to speak"[24]. He tries to remind Umbopa of his place by asking, "What is your name, and where is your kraal? Tell us, that we may know with whom we have to deal"[25]. By asking the young African the location of his kraal, Quatermain attempts to locate him in his own frame of African reference, though Umbopa proves himself beyond this simple system of classification when he says he is "of the Zulu people, yet not of them"[26]. Indeed, he comes from a place the English have never heard of, quite literally beyond their understanding. Faced with such a man, Quatermain confessed he was "rather puzzled" and "mistrusted his offer" because Umbopa was "somehow… different from the ordinary run of Zulus"[27]. Upon meeting a man who falls beyond his experience, Quatermain responds with confusion and mistrust, a mistrust which proves completely unfounded, exposing his ignorance and inability to correctly judge Umbopa at the first.

This is not to say that Quatermain is completely insensitive to racial complexities and the difficulty of empire. On more than one occasion he compares the Africans to the Greeks. For a man whose literary sources appear to be limited to the Old Testament and "The Ingoldsby Legends," this is a rather generous perspective. He describes one young Kukuana as "in

---

[22] Ibid., 165.
[23] Ibid., 6.
[24] Ibid., 34.
[25] Ibid., 34.
[26] Ibid., 34.
[27] Ibid., 36.

the attitude of a Grecian statue of a spear thrower"[28]. When Ignosi addresses the warriors after his victory over Twala, Quatermain compares his speech to Homer: "Once I heard a scholar with a fine voice read aloud from the Greek poet Homer.... Ignosi's chant, uttered as it was in a language as beautiful and sonorous as the old Greek, produced exactly the same effect in me"[29]. With no other point of reference, Quatermain turns to the best speeches he himself has had access to. Throughout the novel, most of the noblest and most poetic speeches are reserved for the African characters.

Throughout the book, Quatermain confesses his admiration for the appearance and courage of the Africans, but then pushes them aside, more comfortable in his familiar way of interpreting the world. In his introduction, he speaks of himself as a man "more accustomed to handle a rifle than a pen"[30] who will record what happened and "leave these matters to be dealt with subsequently in whatever way ultimately may be desirable"[31]. Thus Haggard leaves the events of the novel for the reader to interpret.

As Fuller writes in the introduction to the novel, King Solomon's Mines is ""… the vehicle in which Haggard had set his 'faithful but unpretending record' might comfortably expose Victorian bias and belief for what it was: a thin veneer of racial and gender superiority stretched over the deeper truth of complicated human relations"[32]. We have only to take Quatermain's position as a starting point to understand how the rhetoric shifts away from typical Victorian attitudes through the course of the novel.

## Sir Henry as African Hero

The hero of the battle in Kukuanaland, the slayer of King Twala, and the bravest of the group of white men, Sir Henry Curtis is perhaps as much the hero of the novel as the cleverer yet less martial Alan Quatermain. Therefore, it is telling that Alan Quatermain is put immediately in mind of a very ungentlemanly civilization, the ancient Danes, when he first sees Sir Henry. As the strongest of the group, Sir Henry triumphs in Africa because of his barbaric roots, turning to his savage ancestry in a land where Englishness cannot avail him. While this questions the idea of white supremacy and also the ultimate fate of British imperialism in Africa, it reaffirms the theory of racial essentialism, one which binds ethnic identity to place: the idea that each race has a "proper" place, a geographical location to which it belongs. The English thrive in England but lack an inborn quality that would make them successful in Africa. This quality, one which Africans possess, is

---

[28] Ibid., 82.
[29] Ibid., 175-176.
[30] Ibid., 4.
[31] Ibid., 4.
[32] Ibid., xviii.

supplemented by Sir Henry's atavistic Danish traits, but this only further underscores the association of barbarism and blackness in the novel.

Quatermain goes as far as to equate the Danes with Africans, calling them "a kind of white Zulus"[33]. When Quatermain imagines holding "a battle-axe and a horn mug," this image can be read precisely as the opposite of Victorian ideals of refined masculinity[34]. Between Sir Henry and Captain Good, who is introduced as a Naval officer and therefore a gentleman, Sir Henry is certainly the more effective and less buffoonish character, yet his virtues are more in keeping with African ideals than English. His attitudes toward life can be summed up in his approximation of his plan to find his lost brother: "If we are to be knocked on the head, all I have to say is, that I hope we shall get a little shooting first"[35].

Sir Henry's opinions are echoed by those of Umbopa, later revealed as Ignosi, the rightful king of Kukuanas. He declares, "It is well to try and journey one's road and to fight with the air. Man must die. At the worst he can but die a little sooner"[36]. It is no wonder Umbopa says to Sir Henry, "It seems to me that we are much alike"[37]. They are both heroes of an uncivilized cast.

Quatermain himself appears to subscribe to this thinking, though as an "orderly man" he would never admit it. When he first introduces Sir Henry, the narrator writes, ""I never saw a finer-looking man"[38]. A little later, when describing the breadth of Umbopa's shoulders and his marvelous physique in similar language, he echoes, "I never saw a finer native"[39]. The use of the term "native" here must be noted: even when he uses almost exactly the same language to describe the two men, Quatermain does not explicitly compare Umbopa to white people, reaffirming his separation of races and unconscious belief that one cannot be equated with the other even in physical terms.

At the battle of Loo, Sir Henry fights with the Greys, the regiment of seasoned fighting men who form the vanguard of Ignosi's army and bear more than a passing resemblance to European veteran regiments such as the French Old Guard. At the height of the battle, Sir Henry appears to revert— or perhaps rise—to the level of his barbaric ancestors. After his description of the brave Greys, Quatermain describes Sir Henry: "And yet more gallant was the vision of Sir Henry, whose... long yellow hair streamed out in the breeze behind him. There he stood, the great Dane, for he was nothing else, his hands, his axe, and his armour, all red with blood, and none could live

---

33 Ibid., 8.
34 Ibid., 8.
35 Ibid., 29.
36 Ibid., 50.
37 Ibid., 51.
38 Ibid., 7.
39 Ibid., 36.

before his stroke"[40]. The comparison becomes even more marked shortly: "as he struck he shouted "O-hoy! O-hoy!" like his Berserkir forefathers"[41]. On the field of battle in Africa, without the gatlings whose lack Captain Good bemoans, Sir Henry lets out his inner Norseman and as such finds his place among the Africans, fighting as an equal with them in physical prowess.

The connection between the two, the Englishman and the African, become complete when Sir Henry kills Twala to complete their victory over the old king and place Ignosi in his place. Entreating him not to fight, Ignosi begs, "Fight not, my white brother… if aught befell thee at his hands it would cut my heart in twain"[42]. In Ignosi's poetic words, he is not only Sir Henry's brother, but they appear to share a heart as well. In the life-and-death struggle between him and the king, Captain Good's typically English shouts of, "Go it, old fellow! … Give it him amidships!" is remarkably incongruous, both in its Englishisms and the naval metaphor in the landlocked center of Africa[43]. In Africa, the fury of battle is not dressed in the garb of European culture. Only a man like Sir Henry Curtis, as strong at heart as a Zulu, can triumph in such combat. It is because of his non-Christian, Viking Danish ancestors, whom he channels in the melee, that he, an Englishman, wins the day.

## Captain Good as Symbol of the Limits of English Imperialism

From his first introduction, Captain John Good is presented as a true English gentleman. Quatermain appears satisfied that he has found the true definition of the term: "I asked a page or two back, what is a gentleman? I'll answer it now: a Royal Naval officer is…"[44]. Good is identified not only by his gentlemanly behavior but by the trappings of English gentility: his clothing. The narrator places special emphasis on his eye-glass, which he appears never to remove, even to the point that he believes at first that Good wears it to sleep. This eye-glass is so much a part of Good's identity that "It seemed to grow there [over his eye], as it had no string"[45]. The eye-glass and his clothing thereafter become the defining character traits of Good. It is worth noting that his very name seems to stress his status as a gentleman.

Captain Good reveals the peril of the Englishman attempting to live in Africa without adjusting to native habits. The reader is reminded of the threat of the Zulus to the established European order when Quatermain later mentions the death of "the Prince Imperial," Napoleon Eugene, during the war with the Zulus[46]. This mention comes at the beginning of the incident

---


[40] Ibid., 167.
[41] Ibid., 167.
[42] Ibid., 172.
[43] Ibid., 173.
[44] Ibid., 8.
[45] Ibid., 9.
[46] Ibid., 44.

with the elephants, when the elephant shot by Good charges him. Good's poor shooting sets off the chain of events which is made even more dangerous by his clothing. Quatermain writes that "Good fell a victim to his passion for civilized dress" when his trousers and boots cause him to stumble and fall in the path of the elephant. Because Good insists on dressing in a "civilized" fashion, rather than wearing the clothes more suited to the environment as Quatermain and Sir Henry do, he finds himself in mortal danger.

It is only through the quick action of a native, "Khiva, the Zulu boy," that Captain Good escapes a terrible death[47]. Quatermain describes the boy's death in gory detail when he rushes to aid Good and distract the elephant the naval officer's shot had maddened. Good is moved by the death of the African. The narrator stresses that, in his sacrifice, Khiva was a man, rather than speaking of him in the patronizing imperial terms of "Zulu boy." Quatermain says Good "wrung his hands over the brave man who had given his life to save him"[48]. To underscore the point, Umbopa confirms, "he is dead, but he died like a man"[49]. As a demonstration of their respect for him, they bury Khiva "together with his assegai to protect himself with on his journey to a better world"[50]. The incompetence of the white man's shooting and inability to survive in Africa because of his gentleman's clothing is redeemed only by the loyalty of a native who sacrifices himself for Good. It must be noted that at the heart of this scene is also the fact that a person of color gives his life for a white man, as though acknowledging the superior value of that life, and the scene must be read keeping in mind the internalized racism this reflects.

Having been established as a symbol of the British gentleman in Africa, Captain Good's role rises to ridiculous heights when his accoutrements become the means of both impressing the natives and of reducing him to a parody of a refined Englishman in Africa. When the party is about to be killed by Kukuanas, Good appears, half-shaven, dressed in only shirt, and clicking his false teeth. The old warrior who leads the band, who is later identified as Infadoos, the brother of the former king, is so amazed by Good's appearance that he exclaims, "How is it, O strangers,… that this fat man… whose body is clothed, and whose legs are bare, who grows hair on one side of his sickly face and not on the other, and who wears one shining and transparent eye, has teeth that move of themselves, coming away from the jaws and returning of their own will?"[51] It is only after Quatermain explains that these are signs of their origin among the stars that Infadoos agrees not to kill them, and as a

----

47 Ibid., 45.
48 Ibid., 46.
49 Ibid., 46.
50 Ibid., 47.
51 Ibid., 83.

result, Captain Good is forced to continue to wear this ridiculous ensemble, going with his legs bare and his face half-shaved for the remainder of the adventure. The naval officer, having been established as the definition of an English gentleman, now finds himself playing out a farcical role to appease the image the natives have formed of him.

Far from being an ideal symbol of manliness, Good must repeatedly perform this role to impress the natives. The reader cannot help but read into this the need of the English to play into perceptions of superiority and power. Good's predicament demonstrates the Englishman's necessity to perform the established notions of Englishness even when they are clearly directly opposed to his own well-being and wishes. As Sir Henry explains, "you have appeared in this country in a certain character, and you must live up to it. It will never do to put on trousers again. Henceforth you must exist in a flannel shirt, a pair of boots, and an eye-glass"[52].

Rather than sticking to any class of gentlemanly behavior, Good is forced to rely on his sailor's talent for prodigious swearing when even Quatermain's wit fails during the solar eclipse and only Good is still spouting off his expletives to confuse the natives. Quatermain encourages him, "Keep it up, Good, I can't remember any more poetry. Curse away, there's a good fellow"[53]. In Quatermain's paternalistic tone, the reader can understand the level to which Good has fallen, spouting merely gibberish to impress the locals.

To further underscore the Royal Naval officer, Quatermain's ideal of British manhood, Captain Good is quite obviously feminized by the natives' obsession with his "beautiful white legs," which they ask him to display for them on a number of occasions. Rather than a demonstration of his superiority through the color of his skin, the whiteness of Good's legs proves to be a source of embarrassment. Even after the death of his beloved Foulata, Good is pestered by the Kukuana women to show off his legs. At first, he objects vehemently, exclaiming, "I won't… it is positively indecent" though Sir Henry insists without irony, "you can't refuse to oblige a lady"[54]. As a gentleman, Good is forced to do as the "ladies" ask. In order to behave to the expectations of the natives, Captain Good must transgress his own ideas of decency.

By the end of the adventure, Captain Good has loved and lost the beautiful Foulata, a relationship that will be discussed in the following section. Though Quatermain expresses his relief that the relationship will not prove complicating, the experience has undoubtedly changed Good's opinions of the Africans. Upon parting with Infadoos, he gives the old man his spare eye-glass. By doing so, he bestows on the African the very symbol

---

[52] Ibid., 87.
[53] Ibid., 137.
[54] Ibid., 228.

of his gentlemanliness. The symbolism of the Naval Officer giving his African counterpart the item that has come to symbolize his identity as an English gentleman is obvious to even Quatermain, though the old hunter, as stuck in his ways as ever, remarks in the narration, "Eye-glasses to not go well with leopard-skin cloaks and black ostrich plumes"[55]. Quatermain is nothing if not entrenched in his opinions, while even Sir Henry admits, "I think that there are worse places than Kukuanaland in the world, and that I have known unhappier times than the last month or two, though I have never spent such queer ones"[56]. While Good admits he wishes he were back, Quatermain is more concerned with his own well-being, reflecting on his close shaves.

## Foulata as Tragic Heroine

The women in Haggard novels are frequently dismissed by critics who condemn Haggard for the misogynist content of his novels. One critic, Rebecca Stott, writes "the native woman is usually dispensed with to avoid complications of miscegenation"[57]. She is undoubtedly referring at least in part to Foulata, the heroine of the novel, who is killed by the shriveled witch Gagool when she attempts to stop the old witch from escaping the tomb in which she has trapped the heroes. Stott takes it at face value when Quatermain writes,

> I am bound to say, looking at the thing from the point of view of an oldish man of the world, that I consider her removal was a fortunate occurrence, since, otherwise, complications would have been sure to ensue. The poor creature was no ordinary native girl, but a person of great, I had almost said stately, beauty, and of considerable refinement of mind. But no amount of beauty or refinement could have made an entanglement between Good and herself a desirable occurrence; for, as she herself put it, 'Can the sun mate with the darkness, or the white with the black?'[58]

The description of Foulata's death as "her removal" and a "fortunate occurrence" is shockingly racist, once again demonstrating Quatermain's conscious and unquestioned white supremacist thinking. Added to this is his consistent use of the term "girl" to refer to Foulata, infantilizing her and thus repeating Victorian ideologies about Africans as children incapable of ruling

---

[55] Ibid., 230.

[56] Ibid., 230.

[57] Rebecca Stott, "The Dark Continent: Africa as Female Body in Haggard's Adventure Fiction," *Feminist Review* 32 (1989): 70, accessed February 15, 2017, http://search.ebscohost.com/login.aspx?direct=true&db=edsjsr&AN=edsjsr.10.2307.13953 64.

[58] Haggard, *Somon's Mines,* 222.

themselves. Further review might suggest that these are not the whole of Quatermain's thoughts. Even in this description, Quatermain expresses his intense respect for Foulata, and confesses it is only because he is "an oldish man of the world," and therefore without hope for things to change, that he holds this opinion. A more thorough reading reveals Haggard is much kinder to his heroine than Quatermain's own pronouncement suggests.

The old hunter's perspective is just one among the Englishmen. Captain Good, for his part, remains in love with Foulata even after he returns to England. Quatermain has already proved to be a poor judge of others by his initial distrust of Ignosi. When he dismisses Captain Good's feelings as a "sailor ... falling in love upon the slightest provocation!"[59], he will again prove to be mistaken. After her death, Captain Good finds even English women lacking in comparison.

When Quatermain speaks of Foulata, he does so invariably in deeply affectionate, even openly sentimental terms. When he writes of her fondness and devotion to Good, Quatermain says, without seeming to understand the implication, "I remember my dear wife was just the same"[60]. Quatermain has no trouble speaking of an African woman in the same breath as his wife. When he introduces her, Quatermain writes of his story, "there is no woman in it—except Foulata"[61], and stresses with patriarchal dismissal that the witch Gagool does not count because she is "not marriageable"[62]. The reader can infer, perhaps, that Foulata therefore is marriageable, despite everything Quatermain says to the contrary.

At the fateful moment of her impending execution, he speaks of her in words that pluck at the heart: "And again she wrung her hands, and turned her tear-stained, flower-crowned face to Heaven, looking so lovely in her despair—for she was indeed a beautiful woman—that assuredly the sight of her would have melted the hearts of any less cruel than were the three fiends before us"[63]. He even goes as far as to compare her plea to a moving moment in Shakespeare spoken not only by a white male but a royal: "Prince Arthur's appeal to the ruffians ... was not more touching than that of this savage girl"[64]. Quatermain betrays his true feelings. Here, he does not think as a rational old Englishman, but as a human being.

He has the same response when she faithfully waits by Good's bedside and tends to him after his injuries at the battle of Loo: "during the entire period [of eighteen hours] did this devoted girl sit by him, fearing that if she moved and drew away her hand it would wake him. What she must have

---

[59] Ibid., 184.
[60] Ibid., 184.
[61] Ibid., 6.
[62] Ibid., 6.
[63] Ibid., 135.
[64] Ibid., 135.

suffered from cramp and weariness, to say nothing of want of food, nobody will ever know; ... when at last he woke, she had to be carried away"[65]. Not only does she nurse him with incredible tenderness, Foulata's love also allows her to transcend not only cultural but language differences: "I am bound to say she understood him marvelously as a rule, considering how extremely limited was his foreign vocabulary"[66]. There can be no fault found in Foulata in her devotion, her gentleness, or her beauty, all Victorian ideals of femininity. Through such a remarkably positive description, Quatermain—or perhaps Haggard—invites comparison with European women, who must be found wanting.

Perhaps Foulata's most touching moment is her tragic death. Knowing she has been given her death wound by Gagool, she lies dying in Captain Good's arms and tells him, through Quatermain's translation, "Say that if I live again, mayhap I shall see him [Good] in the Stars and that—I will search them all, though perchance there I should still be black and he would—still be white"[67]. Even in death, Foulata longs to be with Good as she is, and for him to remain as he is. Rather than focusing on her protestation that "the sun may not mate with the darkness," a reader might find hope in her belief that "I have felt as though there were a bird in my bosom, which would one day fly hence and sing elsewhere"[68]. In her hope for delayed happiness between an African and an Englishman to be found in another life, Foulata dares to think that there will be another time when their love will succeed. After all, she does not say that their love cannot come about, but may not, prevented by society rather than nature.

As such, Haggard's heroine is not merely put out from underfoot as an inconvenience, but rather presents a heartbreakingly tragic figure who yet presents a hope of a future in which such a union will be possible. Good himself, far from being merely a fickle sailor, mourns for Foulata after her death. As expressed in Sir Henry's letter: "He told me that since he had been home he hadn't seen a woman to touch her, either as regards her figure or the sweetness of her expression"[69]. Captain Good, for one, has most certainly not "dispensed with" Foulata.

## The Final Chapters

Though it would require a much longer text to examine in depth every chapter of *King Solomon's Mines* for the anti-Imperial rhetoric of its imagery, the final few chapters offer such a remarkable attack on British colonialism

---

[65] Ibid., 183.
[66] Ibid., 183.
[67] Ibid., 208.
[68] Ibid., 208.
[69] Ibid., 235.

that the rest of the novel may be judged by it. Even Norman Etherington, whose 1972 article in *Victorian Studies* contested other readings of Haggard that believed it purely imperialistic, only looked at the text as a journey into the subconscious, but failed to interpret how this deconstructs the imperialist paradigm.

It must be stressed, of course, that Haggard's destabilization of the colonialist imagination is limited by his own experience and ideological experience. Robbie McLaughlan's excellent Re-imagining the 'Dark Continent' examines Dark Continent fiction through the lens of psychoanalysis, treating it, as Etherington does, as a journey into the psyche, yet his analysis also reveals a complex relationship with Africa in both Haggard's writing and his life. McLaughlan uses the example of Haggard's encounter with an "African withdoctor" that leaves him disturbed and wondering whether the man genuinely had supernatural powers. As McLaughlan explains, Haggard's inability to write about and therefore to fully understand the situation "imbues his narratives with a loaded ambiguity, and undermines Haggard's subtle, searching criticisms of the imperial enterprise"[70]. While we can show how Haggard glimpsed and deconstructed elements of imperialist ideology, his own racism and fear of the Other prevented him from fully grasping the scope and awfulness of the constructions he questioned.

Indeed, a closer look reveals suggestions of connections to other novels that problematize European imperialism in Africa. There are echoes of the gouged landscape of Heart of Darkness in the pits that form the diamond mines. It is this hole that Quatermain compares to the vast English diamond mines in Africa[71]. Haggard thus directly equates Solomon's mine with English imperialism. The symbolism of the three Englishmen having to climb back up the slopes of that pit after their ordeal in the cave cannot be missed. After being birthed back into the world through the tunnel they use to escape, they must clamber back up the literal decline which previous colonial enterprises have left on the African landscape in order to once again reach the level of the African nation of Kukuanaland.

The association of the diamond mine with fruitless death is clear in the text. The cave where the diamonds are stored is called "The Place of Death," and is watched over by the "Silent Ones," three deities of three previous civilizations, Zidonians, Moabites, and the children of Ammon, who tried previously to colonize the valley[72]. Now, these crumbling statues are all that remain of those races. Among the nightmarish scenes inside the cave, perhaps the most telling is the grisly scene of the table at which sit the dead

---

[70] Robbie McLaughlan, *Re-imagining the 'Dark Continent' in Fin-de-siecle Literature* (Edinburgh: Edinburgh UP, 2012), 78.
[71] Haggard, *Solomon's Mines*, 16.
[72] Ibid., 191.

kings of the valley, each slowly turning into a stalactite, ruled over by "Death himself, in the form of a colossal human skeleton, fifteen feet or more in height"[73]. Quatermain responds with horror at this sight of the would-be rulers of the valley seated at their eternal table with death: "Anything more awe-inspiring than the spectacle of this long line of departed royalties…, with Death himself for a host, it is impossible to imagine"[74]. Even considering the slow transformation of the dead into stone, the connection to questions of race is obvious in the final exclamation of Quatermain at the end of the chapter: "Such, at any rate, was the White Death and such were the White Dead!"[75]. As again Quatermain reminds the reader to "form his own conclusion," the contemporary English audience was forced to consider their own whiteness in relation to this grisly scene depicting the former rulers of the African nation[76].

Further examining the role of the diamond mines, Gerald Monsman provides a background for Haggard's condemnation of imperialist greed in his article "Of Diamonds and Deities: Social Anthropology in H. Rider Haggard's King Solomon's Mines." He sets the novel against various speeches and other writings by the author, including a 1905 speech in Canada in which Haggard "assert[ed] that the commercial and technological wealth of urban life is valueless apart from an Antaeus-like contact with the land and fertility"[77]. In Haggard's terms, this connection with land is evidenced among people of color, while it has been threatened by urbanization and automatization in Britain. While we must note the connections to myths of the noble savage, this amply demonstrates Haggard's reservations about continuing British imperialist exploitation in Africa.

According to Monsman, Haggard's text encourages "a Kukuanaland uncontaminated by the socio-economic structures of the West"[78]. Far from delighting at their victory, the Englishmen grow to curse the diamonds. Gagool's taunt to the white men to "eat of them, … drink of them!"[79] echoes in their ears when they are trapped with an enormous fortune but about to die of thirst in darkness, and are forced to count their matches for snatches of light. As Quatermain writes, "we should be glad to exchange them [the diamonds] for a bit of food or a cup of water, and, after that, even for the privilege of a speedy close to our sufferings. Truly wealth, which men spend

---

[73] Ibid., 196.

[74] Ibid., 198.

[75] Ibid., 199.

[76] Ibid., 199.

[77] Gerald Monsman, "Of Diamonds and Deities: Social Anthropology in H. Rider Haggard's King Solomon's Mines," *English Literature in Transition, 1880-1920*. 43, no. 3 (2000): 281, accessed February 15, 2017 http://search.ebscohost.com/login.aspx?direct=true&db =a9h&AN=15746761.

[78] Ibid., 288.

[79] Haggard, *Solomon's Mines*, 206.

their lives in acquiring, is a valueless thing at the last"[80]. Gone are any notions of a colonial adventure for wealth. Instead, the men are nauseated by the very thought of the wealth they threw their lives away to collect. It is a sobering statement about the true nature of the imperialist enterprise.

Even when Quatermain's cleverness gives them a chance at escape, and they feel around for a source of air that will lead to an exit, the narrator is reminded of the price they pay: "Presently my ardour received a check. I put my hand on something cold. It was poor Foulata's dead face"[81]. Even when groping for survival out of the bowels of Africa to which his greed has brought him, Quatermain must do it literally over the African dead.

Beyond the death waiting for Africa's conquerors that Gagool promises and the caves demonstrate, the novel offers a last condemnation of the Englishmen's lust for diamonds and conquest at their parting from Ignosi. He speaks sadly of the greed of white men: "Ye have the stones; now ye would go to… sell them, and be rich, as it is the desire of a white man's heart to be. Cursed for your sake be the white stones, and cursed he who seeks them. Death it be to him who sets foot in the place of death to find them"[82]. Beyond his closing of Kukuanaland to all foreigners, save the three Englishmen who now understand to some measure the price of their adventure, Ignosi rejects the things the British would bring to Kukuanaland: "I will see no traders with their guns and their rum. My people shall fight with the spear, and drink water…. I will have no praying-men to put fear of death into men's hearts, to stir them up against the king, and make a path for white men to follow"[83]. And perhaps just as telling is the sober ending with which the white men leave Kukuanaland after such a parting, having no response to such a stern warning: "We went in silence"[84].

## Close

H. Rider Haggard's *King Solomon's Mines* has been interpreted in many ways, many downright dismissive. In 1991, William Scheick wrote, "At the core of his [Haggard's] novel is a joke that yokes male adolescent pornographic fantasies with the misogynist and imperialist impulses of Haggard's imagined audience of 'big and little boys'"[85]. There are elements of Orientalism and melodrama that would have stirred the readers of his day in the novel. A close

---

[80] Ibid., 212.

[81] Ibid., 213.

[82] Ibid., 226.

[83] Ibid., 226.

[84] Ibid., 227.

[85] William J. Scheick, "Adolescent Pornography and Imperialism in Haggard's King Solomon's Mines," *English Literature in Transition, 1880-1920* 34, no. 1 (1991): 20, accessed February 15, 2017, http://search.ebscohost.com/login.aspx?direct=true&db=edspmu&AN=edspmu. S1559271591100025.

reading of the text reveals a story that is aware of the fantasies it employs and deeply critical of the racism and imperialism at the heart of British contemporary foreign policy, while remaining deeply racist and unable to move beyond the essentialist rhetoric at the heart of colonial practice.

After they leave Kukuanaland in somber spirits, the white heroes of the novel encounter one last remarkable coincidence in Africa which adds a final twist to Haggard's tale. They find Sir Henry's brother George, the reason for their quest into the uncharted wilds, alive and living in a hut with Jim, an African hunter with whom he had traveled. According to their story, George has been living there with Jim, laid up with a broken leg and tended to by Jim. Perhaps, at this last, the reader can find one last parallel b[86]etween the story and reality, as the African keeps alive the crippled Englishman, both waiting for the day the white man can leave Africa for good. In this scene, we have again the depiction of a black man as inherently a servant and inferior to a white man, a white man who is out of place and unable to survive on his own in Africa, where the black man belongs.

## Bibliography


Rusty Burke (introduction) in Robert E. Howard, *The Best of Robert E. Howard Volume 2: Grim Lands*, New York: Ballantine Books, 2007.

Etherington, Norman A. "Rider Haggard, Imperialism, and the Layered Personality." *Victorian Studies* 22, no. 1 (1978): 71-87. Accessed February 15, 2017. http://www.jstor.org/stable/3826929

Fuller, Alexandra. Introduction to *King Solomon's Mines*. New York: The Modern Library, 2002.

Haggard, Henry Rider. *King Solomon's Mines*. New York: The Modern Library, 2002.

Kaufman, Heidi. "'King Solomon's Mines?:' African Jewry, British Imperialism, and H. Rider Haggard's Diamonds." *Victorian Literature and Culture* 33, no. 2 (2005): 517-539. Accessed February 15, 2017. http://www.jstor.org/stable/25058726

Monsman, Gerald. "Of Diamonds and Deities: Social Anthropology in H. Rider Haggard's *King Solomon's Mines*." *English Literature in Transition, 1880-1920* 43, no. 3 (2000): 280-297. Accessed February 15, 2017. http://search.ebscohost.com/login.aspx?direct=true&db=a9h&AN=15746761

Nielsen, Leon. *Robert E. Howard: A Collector's Descriptive Bibliography of American and British Hardcover, Paperback, Magazine, Special and Amateur Editions, with a Biography*. London: McFarland & Company, Inc. Publishers, 2007.


---

[86]

Scheick, William J. "Adolescent Pornography and Imperialism in Haggard's *King Solomon's Mines.*" *English Literature in Transition, 1880-1920* 34, no. 1 (1991): 18-30. Accessed February 15, 2017. http://search.ebscohost.com/login.aspx?direct=true&db=edspmu&AN=edspmu.S1559271591100025

Stott, Rebecca. "The Dark Continent: Africa as Female Body in Haggard's Adventure Fiction." *Feminist Review* 32 (1989): 69-89. Accessed February 15, 2017. http://search.ebscohost.com/login.aspx?direct=true&db=edsjsr&AN=edsjsr.10.2307.1395364

Tangri, Daniel. "Popular Fiction and the Zimbabwe Controversy." *History in Africa* 17 (1990): 293-304. Accessed February 15, 2017. http://search.ebscohost.com/login.aspx?direct=true&db=edsjsr&AN=edsjsr.10.2307.3171818

# JEKYLL IS HYDE

Perhaps the most fundamental element in the novel *Strange Case of Dr Jekyll and Mr Hyde* is the nature of the relationship between the title characters. Their connection has become so ingrained in popular culture that the phrase "Jekyll and Hyde" has come to represent everything from multiple personality disorder to a seemingly normal person with a terrible secret life. The reader might be tempted to simply believe Jekyll's own opinion about the identity of Hyde when he says Hyde is "the evil side of my nature."[87] The reading of the story as an examination of a simple duality of good and evil has been a prominent interpretation of the novel since its release, and many recent articles continue to touch briefly on this assumption as fact before delving into examining more minute aspects of the text. As with other similar texts, we can find cultural anxieties and the criticism of contemporary hypocrisy in this story. A closer reading suggests that Hyde and Jekyll are different in physical form only. Jekyll shares Hyde's immoral passions, and Hyde behaves like Jekyll when Jekyll ceases to use that form as a vehicle for his desires. By understanding that these two are not different characters, but rather the same person taking two physical bodies, the reader sees that the evil of Hyde is not unique to his form, but a mask that disguises, for a time, the evil inside Jekyll. Jekyll tries to convince himself that Hyde's behavior is separate from his own to avoid the guilt of Hyde's actions, but he is wrong. The shift in appearance allows Jekyll to give in to his baser desires through the persona of Hyde, but the fundamental interconnectedness of their identities causes his downfall. Jekyll cannot disguise and excuse his actions as Hyde because Hyde is Jekyll.

Daneil L. Wright's essay "'The Prisonhouse of My Disposition': A Study of the Psychology of Addiction in *Dr Jekyll and Mr Hyde*" forms a useful basis for an examination of the novel in terms of addiction. Wright demonstrates the numerous parallels between Jekyll's compulsive behavior and our understanding of addiction. Wright discusses in detail Jekyll's descent along the four stages of addiction.[88] He demonstrates several of Jekyll's behaviors

---

[87] Robert Louis Stevenson, *The Strange Case of Dr Jekyll and Mr Hyde and Other Tales of Terror* (London: Penguin Books, 2003), 58.

[88] Daniel L. Wright, "'The Prisonhouse of My Disposition': A Study of the Psychology of Addiction in Dr. Jekyll and Mr. Hyde," *Studies in the Novel* 26.3 (1994): 257-259, accessed February 21, 2017,

that are typical of an addict, such as drawing others into helping him obtain what he needs for his addiction,[89] distancing himself from friends,[90] and his mistaken belief in his control over his addiction[91] followed by despair at the realization of his helplessness.[92] Though thorough in his analysis, Wright never explicitly details the nature of Jekyll's addiction to Hyde, such as whether it is a psychological or chemical addiction, and from whence it originates. This essay aims to develop this question. By understanding the true relationship between Jekyll and Hyde as two faces of the same man, we can see that Jekyll's addiction stems from his delight at being able to do the things he has always prevented himself from indulging in. The freedom from prosecution and social liability that Hyde offers Jekyll becomes intoxicating, inescapable, and fatal.

The difference in the actions of Jekyll and Hyde is not in morality but in the publicness of them. The level to which either form allows himself to go is dictated not by conscience but by discretion enforced by fear of the consequences of culturally unacceptable action. Though Jekyll wants to behave as Hyde does, fear prevents him from doing so, leaving him "an ordinary secret sinner."[93] While Jekyll, in his original shape, and the rest of London society disguise their immorality, Jekyll-as-Hyde behaves openly. He is able to create a spectacle because his actions cannot be traced back to his original form. By disguising himself again in his reputable shape, Jekyll is able to escape detection—until, of course, he loses control of the transformation.

Even before he creates Hyde, Jekyll engages in vice, though he hides it behind his respectability. One can suppose Jekyll has refrained from committing more than "undignified" pleasures[94] not because of his conscience, but rather because he fears the consequences to his status, freedom, and life. When Jekyll insists his has been "nine tenths a life of effort, virtue, and control,"[95] the reader cannot help but wonder what the remaining tenth was like. Jekyll, after all, gives no accounting of it, inviting the reader's imagination and speculation to fill the gap.

Jekyll shares his enjoyment of "undignified" pleasures with the rest of Victorian London in this novel. He lives in a distinctly immoral society, one that disguises its crimes rather than avoids them. For instance, the narrator introduces Jekyll's friend Utterson in terms of one primary virtue: "he had an approved tolerance for others; sometimes wondering, almost with envy, at

---

http://search.ebscohost.com/login.aspx?direct=true&db=edsglr&AN=edsgcl.15957606257 -259

[89] Ibid., 261-262.

[90] Ibid., 260.

[91] Ibid., 255-256.

[92] Ibid., 260-261.

[93] Stevenson, *Jekyll and Hyde*, 65.

[94] Ibid., 60.

[95] Ibid., 58.

the high pressure of spirits involved in their misdeeds; and in any extremity inclined to help rather than reprove."[96] That Jekyll should have such a lawyer says much about his character. When he confronts Jekyll about his connection with Hyde through the will, Utterson tells him, "Make a clean breast of this in confidence, and I make no doubt I can get you out of it."[97] Here, again, the focus is not on preventing immoral behavior, but on hiding it, exposing the hypocrisy of Utterson, a lawyer. Utterson, nominally a gentleman, is neither indignant nor surprised at Jekyll's admission. It is not the transgression that worries Utterson but that Jekyll can no longer disguise it. After all, when reflecting on Jekyll's crime, Utterson cannot help but think what might come of his own secret crimes: "And the lawyer, scared by the thought, brooded awhile on his own past, groping into all the corners of memory, lest by chance some Jack-in-the-Box of an old iniquity should leap to light there."[98] Utterson's closet has its own skeletons.

The rest of society is equally rotten. Utterson is friends with Mr Enfield, "the well-known man about town," whose own reputation makes their connection "a tough nut to crack for many."[99] The acquaintances of the trampled child, rather than contacting a policeman, blackmail Hyde for a hundred pounds.[100] Even Sir Danvers Carew, a Member of Parliament, goes walking by the river in a bad part of town in the small hours of the morning.[101] Jekyll and his society are far from morally pure; their only pretense at respectability comes from hiding their actions.

It is obvious why Jekyll would want to create a Hyde for himself in a society that values the appearance of propriety while turning a blind eye to the secrets of its members. It is this quality of disguise, not so much a shift in actual personality, which Jekyll stresses as soon as he introduces the idea of separating the sides of a man: "the unjust might go his way, delivered from the aspirations and remorse of his more upright twin; and the just could walk steadfastly and securely on his upward path… no longer exposed to disgrace and penitence at the hands of his extraneous evil."[102] Jekyll does not seek a means to behave immorally, which he already does, but rather a way to avoid the "disgrace and penitence" doing those evil things would cause him. Jekyll even admits he, "now with the most sensitive apprehensions, now with greedy gusto, projected and shared in the pleasures and adventures of Hyde."[103] In a culture in which losing friends and credit are equivalent and

---

96 Ibid., 5.
97 Ibid., 20.
98 Ibid., 17.
99 Ibid., 6.
100 Ibid.,8.
101 Ibid., 21-22.
102 Ibid., 56.
103 Ibid., 63.

even connected threats[104], Jekyll discovers a way to do boldly what everyone does secretly. Hyde, therefore, becomes a vehicle for Jekyll to revel in his sins, rather than a source of those sins in himself.

Perhaps the most obvious instance of Jekyll's evil comes in the disastrous moment in which his immoral thoughts cause him to turn spontaneously into Hyde. Jekyll paves the way by choosing not to destroy Hyde's clothes and belongings, thus demonstrating his secret desire to be Hyde once again.[105] It is Jekyll's thoughts, not Hyde's, which cause the spontaneous transformation: "The animal within me lick[ed] the chops of memory; the spiritual side a little drowsed, promising subsequent penitence, but not yet moved to begin. After all, I reflected, I was like my neighbours; and then I smiled, comparing myself to other men, comparing my active goodwill with the lazy cruelty of their neglect."[106] Jekyll imagines he is no worse than his neighbors, who commit their crimes in secret. By letting himself accept, even take pleasure in, the decaying underside of London society, Jekyll exposes himself to the real immorality of the story: that within the self.

When Jekyll allows himself to realize the existence of an immoral being—a "Hyde"—inside himself, Hyde physically emerges, as Jekyll can no longer pretend he is separate from the loathsome criminal who is hunted throughout the city for murder. The distinction between the mask of Hyde and the reality of Jekyll dissolves. Though he has previously referred to Hyde as "Hyde" in his letter, Jekyll now calls him "I." In fact, as the transformations become even more irresistible, he begins to refer to Jekyll in the third person: "The powers of Hyde seemed to have grown with the sickliness of Jekyll. ... With Jekyll, [hate] was a thing of vital instinct. He had now seen...."[107] Perhaps most tellingly of all, it is as Hyde that Jekyll meets his end.[108] Once his crimes have become public, he can no longer disguise the evil inside himself as the other men in the story do.

Just as the immorality in this story stems from Jekyll and not Hyde, Hyde's behavior is not pure evil, and reveals more of Jekyll than the doctor is willing to admit. The very first indication of this is Hyde's behavior after he runs over the little girl, when he is confronted by Enfield and the child's family. Though Hyde's first reaction is "perfectly cool,"[109] perhaps confident that his disguise will protect him from any indemnity, his behavior changes when he is threatened with social and financial repercussions. Realizing his actions might have consequences after all, Hyde replies, "No gentleman but wishes

---

[104] Ibid., 8.
[105] Ibid., 63.
[106] Ibid., 66.
[107] Ibid., 68-69.
[108] Ibid., 45.
[109] Ibid., 7.

to avoid a scene"[110] and pays a hundred pounds to keep the matter hidden. While Hyde's behavior is clearly motivated by self-preservation rather than remorse, his concern for his wealth and status is more akin to Jekyll's behavior than Hyde's, whom Jekyll describes as "wholly evil."[111] It is after all Jekyll who seeks to disguise his indiscretions, but here Hyde does the same.

Hyde's efforts to protect Jekyll's reputation become even more pronounced and less apparently evil as the story goes on. After he can no longer access the chemicals necessary to transform back into Jekyll, Hyde writes a letter to Dr. Lanyon in which he asks him to bring him the ingredients for the antidote, addressing Lanyon as "one of my oldest friends"[112] and signing it, "Your friend, H.J."[113] One can hardly imagine an "ape-like" Hyde writing such an eloquent and desperate letter, particularly since it involves the destruction of Hyde's own self by Jekyll acquiring the antidote to the formula. The reader can understand the reason Hyde writes so convincingly as Jekyll because there is, in fact, no difference between them except physically.

Particularly toward the end of his life, Hyde's behavior becomes completely that of Jekyll, and there is nothing left of the evil persona Jekyll wants to see in Hyde. If, as Jekyll writes, "all other faculties were most unequally shared" between Jekyll and Hyde,[114] Hyde would be unable to perform Jekyll's chemical procedures. These fail not because he is incompetent but because there is an impurity lacking. Jekyll's assertion that Hyde is "relentless like a man of stone" is completely undermined by the evidence of his grief upon having to face the consequences of his actions.[115] When Poole listens to Hyde's desperate weeping, he describes it as, "Weeping like a woman or a lost soul. … I came away with that upon my heart, that I could have wept too."[116] The butler's sympathetic reaction to Hyde's emotional state also reveals that Hyde has lost something of the repulsive effect he had on others before, when his very presence made others shudder. After the distinction between Jekyll and Hyde becomes broken down, Hyde is no longer just a mask for Jekyll to wear when he wants to indulge his desires. Hyde is Jekyll, and so he not only experiences Jekyll's grief and despair but also demonstrates his humanity. While Jekyll chose to channel his immorality through Hyde, he was monstrous. Now that he has no choice but to be Hyde, Jekyll's real personality comes through.

---

[110] Ibid., 8.
[111] Ibid., 59.
[112] Ibid., 48.
[113] Ibid., 49.
[114] Ibid., 63.
[115] Ibid., 60.
[116] Ibid., 44.

It is therefore not a separate persona, but Jekyll himself in merely an altered form, who cries out, "Utterson… for God's sake, have mercy!" and drinks poison when he realizes he is about to be discovered by Utterson and Poole.[117] Hyde, physically young and powerful, might have forced his way out past a middle-aged lawyer and servant, but chooses instead to destroy himself. When it becomes obvious that he has no more hope of returning to his former appearance as Jekyll, he must face that his secret will become known and the separation in responsibility and guilt he sought to create by using Hyde will dissolve, and Hyde's crimes will fall squarely on the man who is both Jekyll and Hyde. It is that secret, not his impending trial and execution for murder, which drives Hyde to suicide. As Jekyll writes in his final note, "It was no longer the fear of the gallows, it was the horror of being Hyde that racked me."[118] The phrasing here is telling. Jekyll does not only fear becoming or appearing as Hyde, but being him. The real horror is that he is Hyde.

As I have mentioned, it is fear of the guilt and responsibility for Hyde's actions that causes Jekyll to attempt to convince himself and his readers that Hyde's behavior is contrary to his own desires. It is worth noting that the insistence of separation between the two personas comes from Jekyll's letter rather than the objective narrator. Jekyll's "Full Statement" serves as a final attempt to distance himself from his actions by insisting "It was Hyde, after all, and Hyde alone, that was guilty."[119] The reader is already aware of Hyde's human emotions when Jekyll makes his claims to the contrary, rendering Jekyll's testimony immediately hollow.

Perhaps Jekyll wants Hyde to be evil when he creates the elixir, but he is not. Jekyll merely succeeds in creating another face for himself, complete with his full moral complexity and awareness. As Harriet Hustis explains, "The holistic Hyde to which Jekyll attests clearly fails to embody the moral dissociation—the separate housing—that he seeks."[120] Despite failing to create a separate and pure self, Jekyll insists he has done so, in order to distance himself from Hyde's evil actions. "To the extent that Hyde represents a projection of Jekyll's bifurcated identity, Hyde's 'evil' would necessarily be commingled with Jekyll's 'good'—a possibility that his 'Full Statement' is determined to erase or overwrite."[121] By presenting Hyde as a separate entity in his letter, he denies that Hyde's actions were his own.

---

[117] Ibid., 44.
[118] Ibid., 68.
[119] Ibid., 60.
[120] Harriet Hustis, "Hyding Nietzsche in Robert Louis Stevenson's Gothic of Philosophy," *SEL: Studies in English Literature 1500-1900* 49.4 (2009): 1003, accessed February 21, 2017, doi: 10.1353/sel.0.0074.
[121] Ibid., 1003.

The reader might wonder why, if Jekyll and Hyde are the same person, Hyde becomes physically larger as his actions become more and more diabolical. If we believe Jekyll's claim that Hyde is initially smaller of frame than Jekyll because Jekyll's evil side "had been much less exercised and much less exhausted"[122] than his good, and his later fear that Hyde "had grown in stature,"[123] we might conclude, as Jekyll does, that Hyde grows larger by exercise almost as a muscle does. It can be understood, however, that this physical change is a product of Jekyll's own fearful imagination rather than a fact. Jekyll says it *"seemed to me* as of late as though the body of Edward Hyde had grown in stature."[124] Jekyll later again describes Hyde's smaller stature after his transformation: "my clothes hung formlessly on my shrunken limbs," so there has been no great change in Hyde's actual physical size.[125]

A reader might also argue that the need for ever greater doses of the potion to return Jekyll to his original form, combined with the increasing ease of becoming Hyde, demonstrates the slide from Jekyll's balanced self into Hyde's evil as Hyde's evil compounds. This can, however, also be understood as a physical change. The more Jekyll imbibes the formula to become Hyde, the more he shifts toward that form. This is examined at length by Allen MacDuffie, who associates the transformation in the novel with scientific advances in the understanding of thermodynamics in the nineteenth century. He writes that Stevenson "came from a family of engineers, was himself trained as an engineer, and whose earliest published work includes a paper presented to the Royal Society of Edinburgh, 'On the Thermal Influence of Forests.'"[126] MacDuffie describes the slow shift in energy between the two characters, elaborating on the marked decrease in Jekyll's energy as Hyde becomes more lively.[127] Jekyll's gradual shift into Hyde is a result, according to MacDuffie's article, of the first law of thermodynamics and the loss of energy in any transfer.[128] According to this theory, it is science, not morality, that is responsible for this change.

Likewise, Jekyll's horror at Hyde's actions upon returning to his original form might also be explained naturally. Jekyll's reaction may be read as the regret of a murderer who, after acting in a fit of rage, suddenly realizes the degree of the evil he has done. Jekyll's gladness that he is free from

---


[122] Stevenson, *Jekyll and Hyde*, 58.

[123] Ibid., 62.

[124] Ibid., 62, my emphasis.

[125] Ibid., 66.

[126] Allen MacDuffie, "Irreversible Transformations: Robert Louis Stevenson's 'Dr. Jekyll and Mr. Hyde' and Scottish Energy Science," *Representations* 96 (2006): 2, accessed February 21, 2017, doi: 10.1525/rep.2006.96.1.1, 2.

[127] Ibid., 5-6.

[128] Ibid., 7.

prosecution so long as he never again takes the form of Hyde also undermines his remorse about the murder.[129]

This reading of *Strange Case of Dr Jekyll and Mr Hyde* suggests the novel's central theme is one of disguised evil. Stevenson describes a London society concerned with the appearance of propriety rather than with true goodness. The characters of the novel hide their immorality behind a facade of secrets, and Dr Jekyll creates a disguise through which he can indulge in his most wicked passions without fear of consequences. Though he wants to believe he is merely letting a separate, evil version of himself free, it is Jekyll's own desires that Hyde acts on. The thrill of freedom from societal mores becomes irresistible to Jekyll, who struggles with this addiction to Hyde, which is really an addiction to pleasure and giving in to every impulse that Victorian society has taught him to repress. When faced with the impending discovery of his disguise and the revelation that Jekyll is Hyde, he chooses to commit suicide rather than face the consequences, both personal and social, that his Hyde persona has allowed him to temporarily escape. Like many addicts, he comes face to face with the reality that there is no separation between his public life and the secret life of indulging his addiction. Thus, the novel becomes a dark condemnation of a morally corrupt London society in which any seemingly respectable gentleman may become a murderer if the opportunity to do so without consequences presents itself. This interpretation welcomes examining the novel through historical contexts, studying the complex nature of Victorian morality and culture. Though Jekyll attempts to escape society's reproof, it becomes his undoing. As Jekyll writes, "I have been made to learn that the doom and burden of our life is bound forever on a man's shoulders, and when the attempt is made to cast it off, it but returns upon us with more unfamiliar and more awful pressure."[130] This does not only offer a clear insight into Freud's model of the uncanny, it also demonstrates the damage that hypocritical moral outrage causes: while all of the characters in the novel are familiar with the illicit activities that London provides, they keep these actions a nominal secret while condemning those who are discovered. Thus, Jekyll, through his addiction to another body that promises freedom from this constant need for vigilance and secrecy, exposes and destroys himself.

---

[129] Stevenson, *Jekyll and Hyde*, 65.
[130] Ibid., 56.

## Bibliography


Hustis, Harriet. "Hyding Nietzsche in Robert Louis Stevenson's Gothic of Philosophy." *SEL: Studies in English Literature 1500-1900* 49.4 (2009): 993-1007. Accessed February 21, 2017. doi: 10.1353/sel.0.0074.

MacDuffie, Allen. "Irreversible Transformations: Robert Louis Stevenson's 'Dr. Jekyll and Mr. Hyde' and Scottish Energy Science." *Representations* 96 (2006): 1-20. Accessed February 21, 2017. doi: 10.1525/rep.2006.96.1.1.

Stevenson, Robert Louis. *The Strange Case of Dr Jekyll and Mr Hyde and Other Tales of Terror*. London: Penguin Books, 2003.

Wright, Daniel L. "'The Prisonhouse of My Disposition': A Study of the Psychology of Addiction in Dr. Jekyll and Mr. Hyde." *Studies in the Novel* 26.3 (1994): 254-267. Accessed February 21, 2017. http://search.ebscohost.com/login.aspx?direct=true&db=edsglr&AN=edsgcl.15957606

# ANXIETIES OF CLASS AND SEX EXPRESSED IN ARTHUR MACHEN'S *THE GREAT GOD PAN*

In his time Arthur Machen was counted among the fashionable Decadents and created a public stir with his work. Kirsten MacLeod discusses Machen as one of the writers of the Keynote series of books published by Bodley Head publications, which put out his shocking novella *The Great God Pan*. This series, together with the publisher's magazine, the *Yellow Book*, was perceived by its critics as threatening "a large-scale degradation of literature"[131]. The backlash against it by the literary elite may be associated with later criticisms of the weird tale. As MacLeod explains, "much Decadent fiction did indeed combine popular and high art and this disturbed critics at a time when issues of access were of paramount concern in literary debates"[132]. The same could be said for weird fiction, though it has not been said enough.

Machen's twentieth-century fans include such writers as H. P. Lovecraft and Stephen King. In his book *The Weird Tale*, S. T. Joshi examines Machen's work, particularly *The Great God Pan*, as a precursor to Lovecraft's work, paying particular attention to the use of what would be called cosmic horror in the text. There is another way it can be seen to serve as a foundation for the evolution of the weird tale: in its use of its weird plot to explore contemporary cultural anxieties.

A closer look at his novella The Great God Pan reveals a fascinating and adroit treatment of Victorian decadence amid rising anxieties about the subjection of women and the working classes. A bizarre surgery sets events in motion which disturb the accepted order of society. As the illusion of the hierarchy of class and sex is destroyed by access to hidden knowledge, madness, violence, and chaos erupt across both the sordid London alleys and the West End drawing rooms. The worlds of poverty and oppression the middle and upper classes tried to hide away return with full vengeance as the separation between high class and low, men and women falls into violent ruin.

---

[131] Kirsten MacLeod, *Fictions of British Decadence: High Art, Popular Writing, and the* Fin de Siecle, (New York: Palgrave Macmillan, 2006), 116.
[132] Ibid., 117.

The story begins with Mr. Clarke and Dr. Raymond preparing the operation on Dr. Raymond's wife, Mary, which will open her mind to what Raymond calls "The Great God Pan," or the unfettered truth of reality and creation: "the real world" which is hidden from the eyes of humans[133]. The emphasis on repressed and withheld knowledge is clear as he describes the procedure: "I do not know if any human being has ever lifted that veil, but I do know, Clarke, that you and I shall see it lifted this very night from before another's eyes"[134]. Raymond talks about the surgery in terms of exploration, describing it as traveling to "a whole world, a sphere unknown; continents and islands, and great oceans in which no ship has sailed"[135]. As a man of science who has the privilege of being white, educated, and male, Raymond believes in his inherent ability to conquer any frontier with imperialistic force, even that of the imagination.

The two men share a view of Mary as a piece of property fitting to be experimented on, demonstrating their moral bankruptcy. When Clarke raises his doubts about the operation, he does so out of concern for Raymond, not Mary: "Something might go wrong; you would be a miserable man for the rest of your days"[136]. Raymond insists that he has complete control over Mary as though she were a piece of property, a control which he derives both from his sex and his superior social and economic position: "As you know, I rescued Mary from the gutter, and from almost certain starvation, when she was a child; I think her life is mine, to use as I see fit"[137]. The pair have decided not to undergo the operation themselves, but to force it on the unsuspecting Mary, emphasizing their privilege and the recklessness of their pursuit.

This choice to expose Mary to the horrors of the unbridled truth sets off a chain of events that brings tragedy and scandal to London. As an exploited lower-class woman, Mary is in the most helpless position of society. Because she is so victimized, the procedure's goal of revealing the full truth of the world, where socially imposed distinction has put her into the position of test subject for the amusement of wealthy men, must be particularly awful for her. As the knowledge fills her, the agony is described in gruesome detail: "[Mary's eyes] shone with an awful light, looking far away, and a great wonder fell upon her face, ... but in an instant the wonder faded, and gave place to the most awful terror. The muscles of her face were hideously convulsed, she

---

[133] Arthur Machen, *The Caerleon Edition of the Works of Arthur Machen* (London: M. Secker, 1923), 4.

[134] Ibid., 4.

[135] Ibid., 6.

[136] Ibid., 8.

[137] Ibid., 8.

shook from head to foot; the soul seemed struggling and shuddering within the house of flesh"[138].

The forbidden knowledge has destroyed Mary's mind and left her in an empty state. "She was lying wide-awake, rolling her head from side to side, and grinning vacantly. Dr. Raymond regards the results of his experiment with professional detachment. "Yes,' said the doctor, still quite cool, 'it is a great pity; she is a hopeless idiot. However, it could not be helped; and, after all, she has seen the Great God Pan'"[139]. The Great God Pan is said to be a universal concept of knowledge of the unknown, represented by the mythological faun. Any human inkling of love or equitability in the marriage is shattered; Raymond is shielded from the cruelty of his experiment performed on his own wife by his inborn belief that he is by nature superior in sex and class.

Mary's madness and death are later recounted, as well as the existence child she bears after being exposed to the Great God Pan. When the child, Helen, is introduced, Clarke--who is narrating at the time--stresses that she has been kept ignorant: "her guardians need be at no trouble in the matter of education, as she was already sufficiently educated for the position in life which she would occupy"[140]. Yet Helen has been profoundly affected by the knowledge her mother, like a twisted version of Eve, was forced to learn. Helen herself becomes a being of pure destruction.

It becomes immediately clear that Helen lives beyond the boundaries of Victorian morality. She is at once disturbing and powerful. Her budding sexuality, made all the more monstrous by her youth, is shown in revels with a strange figure in the forest. A boy of the village observes "Helen V. playing on the grass with a 'strange naked man,' who he seemed unable to describe more fully"[141]. The boy is struck with horror at the sight of this "man," whom he later identifies with an antique Roman bust of a satyr: "a curious head, evidently of the Roman period, which had been placed in the manner described. The head is pronounced by the most experienced archaeologists of the district to be that of a faun or satyr"[142]. This is notably similar to representations of the devil. In this recurring figure, the titular "Great God Pan," the story combines the threat of pre-Christian pagan religion with understanding beyond Victorian conventions and the demonic influence said to be lurking in the wild woods. His appearance leaves those who see him maddened, corrupted, or both.

Helen's first act is to penetrate class boundaries and corrupt a young woman of her own age, leading her into carnal knowledge. She chooses her

---

[138] Ibid., 13.
[139] Ibid., 13-14.
[140] Ibid, 18.
[141] Ibid., 20.
[142] Ibid., 22.

companion, Rachel, "the daughter of a prosperous farmer"[143]. Despite the visible influence Helen has on Rachel, her parents do not interfere, as they see Helen as a potential means of financial profit through their friendship: "the impression was general that she [Helen] would one day inherit a large sum of money from her relative. The parents of Rachel were therefore not averse from their daughter's friendship with the girl, and even encouraged the intimacy, though they now bitterly regret having done so"[144]. Rachel's parents' class aspirations, coupled with their belief that no one from a wealthy family could be a bad influence, seal her fate.

When Clarke learns that Helen has led Rachel to a forested pagan ruin and, it is suggested, made her a victim of the lusts of the Great God Pan, he responds by trying to repress what he has heard. He frames his response in terms of the stability of society, which is now threatened by the knowledge coming to life in Helen. "Why, man, if such a case were possible, our earth would be a nightmare"[145]. The truth of what happened in the forest is so heinous it is only revealed at the end of the story, the final blow: "And into this pleasant glade Rachel passaged a girl, and left it, who shall say what?"[146]. After Rachel has thus been ruined, Helen leaves her family.

The next part of the story explores the hypocrisy of decadent and debauched London men, who dress and behave like gentlemen but speak boldly of their revels in the city's dens. Thus, they betray the Victorian ideals of respectability and decency, speaking to each other candidly of their misdeeds. By combining the wealth and luxury of the wealthy with the lechery of the poor, the gentlemen place themselves in danger of destroying the distinction between the classes. Helen, now in the dual role of both a wealthy and fashionable society lady and a popular prostitute, is therefore able to destroy a number of them systematically, breaking down the social barriers with her double life.

The dual nature of the lives of the men is revealed in the comparison between Villiers and Charles Herbert, whom Helen has corrupted and driven to absolute ruin through their marriage. They are described in stark contrast: "the one in dirty, evil-looking rags, and the other attired in the regulation uniform of a man about town, trim, glossy, and eminently well-to-do"[147]. As he tells Villiers about the knowledge he has been exposed to, his former friend retreats to the protection of his status. "'…Yes, seen. I have seen the incredible, such horrors that even I myself sometimes stop in the middle of the street and ask whether it is possible for a man to behold such things and

---

[143] Ibid., 23.
[144] Ibid., 23.
[145] Ibid., 24.
[146] Ibid., 85.
[147] Ibid., 26.

live.....' 'But your property, Herbert? You had land in Dorset'"[148]. Villiers, rather than considering the implication of what Herbert is telling him, is interested in Herbert's property, insisting that his wealth and status must protect him from ruin. It does not; Herber has lost it all to Helen.

The narrative stresses the decadence of the middle-class men who form London's elite. When a body is found in the street, it is found by "a gentleman, whose business or pleasure, or both, made him a spectator of the London streets at five o'clock in the morning"[149]. The narrative emphasizes the scandal, not of the death, but of a so-called gentleman being in that part of the city--and this becoming public knowledge: "it struck most people that Paul Street was not exactly the place to look for country gentry"[150]. When Clarke returns to his narration, he speaks of the desire for Helen as a sinful addiction. In his mind, exploring deviant sexuality and exploring the uncanny are strongly connected. He writes of his attempts to set aside his research into the supernatural, titled "Memoirs to prove the existence of the Devil," and "he [Clarke] cherished hopes of a complete self-reformation"[151]. And yet he is strangely drawn to the suggestion of things beyond his understanding. He later writes: "I am like a traveller who has peered over an abyss, and has drawn back in terror. What I know is strange enough and horrible enough, but beyond my knowledge there are depths and horrors more frightful still"[152]. He is both horrified and fascinated by both sexual and supernatural knowledge, which to him are very nearly the same.

As Helen's influence takes hold, a string of wealthy men commit suicide by hanging themselves. The narrator stresses that the crimes in the fashionable West End now mirror those in the sordid East End, referencing the gruesome Jack the Ripper killings. "The police had been forced to confess themselves powerless to arrest or to explain the sordid murders of Whitechapel; but before the horrible suicides of Piccadilly and Mayfair they were dumbfounded" (sic), for not even the mere ferocity which did duty as an explanation of the crimes of the East End, could be of service in the West"[153]. The separation of the upper and lower classes has become collapsed. The horrors of the rookeries spread to the fashionable estates. Austin, Villiers's friend, emphasizes that the Other seems to have become one with the familiar: "The only sensation I can compare it [Helen's power] to, is that odd feeling one sometimes has in a dream, when fantastic cities

---

[148] Ibid., 29-30.
[149] Ibid., 32.
[150] Ibid., 34.
[151] Ibid., 38.
[152] Ibid., 48.
[153] Ibid., 59.

and wondrous lands and phantom personages appear familiar and accustomed"[154].

The control of knowledge has completely shifted from the privileged class to Helen, now going by the title Mrs Beaumont, by the time her role as prostitute becomes known. Villiers procures a packet of documents which detail the sordid debauches she engages in. "Look at this neat little packet of manuscript... It has almost a legal air, hasn't it? ... It is an account of the entertainment Mrs Beaumont provided for her choicer guests"[155]. In a complete reversal, it is the "gentleman" Austin who is unable to bring himself to face the knowledge within: "Austin took the manuscript, but never read it"[156].

MacLeod comments on the control of knowledge in the text, and suggests that the reader is "titillated" twice by the suggestion of what could have happened in the woods, but is twice denied[157]. MacLeod explains this as a way to "make an otherwise unpublishable story publishable" [158], though the gaps play an even more powerful role in the story. As Bakhtin explains, "The word in living conversation is directly, blatantly, oriented toward a future answer-word: it provokes an answer, anticipates it and structures itself in the answer's direction"[159]. *The Great God Pan* does this particularly well with its prurient suggestions of what its readers would have called indecency—but which the text simultaneously shows those readers understand all too well. The text anticipates this knowledge, and relies on it to make its meaning.

Helen herself is a gap in the text, the lack that drives the plot. Though a great deal of text is produced about her, she herself is absent, the lacuna that, like a black hole, creates a driving force that simultaneously moves the text and draws others into oblivion. Helen's role as destabilizer is physically demonstrated in her death. As she dies--forced to strangle herself or let her secret be revealed to the police--her body shifts from form to form, becoming fluid and losing the coherence of a set shape, just as she has crossed all other boundaries of sex, class, and station. "I saw the form waver from sex to sex, dividing itself from itself, and then again reunited. Then I saw the body descend to the beasts whence it ascended, and that which was on the heights go down to the depths, even to the abyss of all being"[160]. Thus, Helen literally breaks down all barriers of separation, destroying the illusion of any

---

[154] Ibid., 62.

[155] Ibid., 74.

[156] Ibid., 75.

[157] MacLeod, *British Decadence*, 127.

[158] Ibid., 127.

[159] Mikhail Bakhtin, *The Dialogic Imagination: Four Essays* (Austin: University of Texas Press, 1982), 180.

[160] Machen, *Great God Pan*, 81.

difference in body and even of the distinction of humans and the animals from which they evolved. All hierarchy is shattered.

At the end of the story, Dr. Raymond reflects on the wrongs he committed. He still does not admit that he wronged his wife, but rather sees that he exposed her to awareness she was never meant to have. "It was ill work I did that night when you were present; I broke open the door of the house of life, without knowing or caring what might pass forth and enter in"[161]. This is the knowledge that destroyed so many lives. Raymond's words echo the importance of the hierarchy created by ideology, and the destructive force that arises from the breakdown of those boundaries. "What I said Mary would see, she saw, but I forgot no human eyes could look on such a vision with impunity. And I forgot, as I have just said, that when the house of life is thus thrown open, there may enter in that for which we have no name"[162]. At the end of the story, Helen and Mary are both dead, but the white male characters are left with their legacy; they now can imagine the full horror of the truth: the fragility of the world they live in, based on a limited understanding of the relationship between the classes and sexes.

Beyond this, the function of the story itself has revealed this to the readers: that they not only understand this horror, but that they already understood it, that it is their own hypocritical knowledge of vice and also of the artificiality of divisions based on gender and class that makes their reading possible.

## Bibliography

Bakhtin, Mikhail. *The Dialogic Imagination: Four Essays*. Austin: University of Texas Press, 1982.

Machen, Arthur. *The Caerleon Edition of the Works of Arthur Machen*. London: M. Secker, 1923.

MacLeod, Kirsten. *Fictions of British Decadence: High Art, Popular Writing, and the Fin de Siècle*. New York: Palgrave Macmillan, 2006.

---

[161] Ibid., 87.
[162] Ibid., 87.

# "AGAINST THE COMPLACENCY OF AN ORTHODOX SUN-DWELLER": THE LOVECRAFT CIRCLE AND THE "WEIRD CLASS"

## *WEIRD TALES* AND THE FORMATION OF THE "WEIRD CLASS"

As the *Weird Tales* writers who became known as the Lovecraft Circle corresponded with one another,[163] they created not only friendships but a cohesive group that consciously set itself apart from the established literary intelligentsia of their age. Their sense of being outsiders and of having been closed out from traditionally legitimate circles appears throughout the writings of this group, reflecting their own position in literary society. In their letters[164] and in the pages of the magazine they wrote for, these writers consciously developed their own separate literary tradition, which was opposed to what was prevalent in the broader world of literature at the time.[165] This chapter will explore what factors led *Weird Tales* in general and

---

[163] Considering the myriad writers who contributed to *Weird Tales*, it is best not to make sweeping claims about all of them, though certain patterns do emerge. Therefore, I will try to focus on the writers of the Lovecraft Circle, though I will also draw general cultural lines from the ongoing conversation in "The Eyrie," which formed the crux of communication among weird fiction enthusiasts. Certainly, the Lovecraft Circle was a key part of that conversation.

[164] Lovecraft kept a voluminous correspondence. S. T. Joshi estimates that he wrote between forty-two thousand and eighty-four thousand letters. "By the 1930s HPL had become a fixture in the worlds of pulp fiction and fantasy fandom, and he accordingly began corresponding with a great many fellow writers." He wrote around 250,000 words in total to Robert E. Howard alone; Howard wrote 300,000 to Lovecraft. S. T. Joshi and David E. Schultz, *An H. P. Lovecraft Encyclopedia* (Westport, CT: Greenwood Press, 2001), 146.

[165] It would be remiss of me not to mention that it has been argued by others that *Weird Tales* and pulp literature in general were influenced by and reflected modernist aesthetics. In this way, it also served to "Make it new!" in a way that destabilized the perception of realism. David Earle and Jason Carney, discussed in this chapter, develop this point very well. Carney shows that the marginalization of the Weird Tales writers allowed them to create this oppositionality, which was a shadow version of what the modernists were doing: "It was the Weird Tales writers' exile from the garden of authentic aesthetic production on a literary plane into the shadows that conditioned and intensified their project." Jason Carney, "The Shadow

the Lovecraft Circle in particular to adopt this outsider status as a "weird class," and it will explore the influence of this new literary culture by highlighting some of the varying ways in which these themes appear in the works of the Lovecraft Circle. To them, the weird tale represented both an escape from a society in which they felt like literary and social outsiders and a path into a common kinship with others who shared their taste in imaginative stories.

*Weird Tales* had a unique place in the field of literature as both pulp fiction and a publication of weird fiction. The magazine was forced to find a compromise—not always a happy one—between selling copies and supporting quality literature. This circumstance and the unique genre of the weird tale, particularly as practiced by the Lovecraft Circle, contributed to the creation and reification of a separate aesthetic that privileged the ability to create uncanny effects. In representing their literary tradition, these writers traced their genre to such respected authors as Arthur Conan Doyle, H. G. Wells, Mary Shelley, and—particularly—Edgar Allan Poe, thus demonstrating their continuity with established literary greatness. They then established the values of their society in their own works. The solidifying of this weird society can be observed in the writers and readers of *Weird Tales* in general, but I will look more closely at the way these ideas appear in the writings of the so-called Lovecraft Circle, as this group of writers consciously and explicitly wrote to one another using their unique aesthetic. The Lovecraft Circle contrasted their stories with those of mainstream literary authors, whom they labeled mundane, unimaginative, and unable to appreciate the sublime thrill that uncanny tales produce on an appropriately sensitive reader. While this aesthetic privileged the *Weird Tales* reader, it particularly honored writers able to produce this effect.

As the writings of the weird class are more closely examined, a hierarchy begins to emerge, one that privileges literary ability and imagination where other class structures favor social power and wealth—traditional advantages from which many of these writers felt cut off, often unfairly so. Edgar Allan Poe can be said to be at the top of the weird class; his stories are used as the standard by which all others were judged. Lovecraft himself figures as, perhaps, Poe's heir,[166] particularly in the eyes of the Lovecraft Circle. He also forms the nexus of that richly varied group of writers through his voluminous letter writing and conscious efforts to encourage writers and introduce them

---

Modernism of Weird Tales: Experimental Pulp Fiction in the Age of Modernist Reflection" (PhD diss., Case Western Reserve University, 2014), 149–50.

[166] The inimitable Gertrude Hemken writes in the December 1937 issue: "The more I read of Lovecraft's work, the more I see in them the modern Poe—by his minute detail of every angle—the history of the family which built the house—the exact description of the plot of ground in which this ancient dwelling stood . . .—on such things I find HPL so very like Poe." See Gertrude Hemken, "Here It Is," *Weird Tales*, December 1937, 760.

to one another. Though Seabury Quinn's Jules de Grandin stories are more popular in his time and more prolific, the praise Lovecraft receives from his contemporaries,[167] not to mention his influence as the head of the Circle, mark him as the peak of weird aristocracy. The rest of the shape of this society takes form in letters and anecdotes: readers tell of traveling to meet with their favorite writers with the same breathless language as explorers visiting sages in exotic lands. Their habits, adventures, and eccentricities are described in adoring detail, creating larger-than-life characters who are the only ones who could craft such wild stories of bizarre imagination, at least in the minds of their admirers.

We can see the interest the members of the weird class take in one another in their letters to one another and to "The Eyrie."[168] The language they use mirrors that of society columns introducing the who's who of a rich culture, and they share stories of one another with a sense of recording the lived lives of literary masters. As an example, Lovecraft writes of a visit from a young protégé thus: "Very shortly I may have another & a longer-term visitor in the person of one of the 'gang's' youngest members—Donald Wandrei of St. Paul, Minn., who turned 21 this summer. He has been working for a year in the advertising dept. of Dutton's in New York."[169] In a time when writers first encountered one another as a name attached to a work, personal stories about the backgrounds of different authors were exchanged with fascination.

The struggle between these opposed aesthetic viewpoints plays out in their stories. In weird fiction, this conflict between the mundane and the imaginative is framed in terms of access to cosmic understanding: being able to imagine a world beyond the accepted one gives characters the capacity to see things as they truly are. These characters can, therefore, accurately perceive truth, as the medium of weird fiction allows the authors to create fictive versions of our own world in which the supernatural, though hidden, is very real. In these stories, there genuinely are worlds of cosmic wonder and terror, and the characters who can perceive them as they are gain power by this or are imperiled by it; frequently both. In this cosmology, society at large

---

[167]In countless instances, one finds sentiments such as those of Harold S. Farnese in the July 1937 issue, which bore memorials to Lovecraft after his death: "But has it ever occurred to you that in Lovecraft you had the greatest genius that ever lived in the realm of weird fiction?" Harold S. Farnese, "The Greatest Genius," *Weird Tales*, July 1937, 125.

[168] As an example, Robert Bloch writes of his fellow authors in "The Eyrie" of September 1934: "No one can claim a more interesting career than [E. Hoffmann] Price, soldier of fortune, etc.; Howard, a typical barbarian like his own Conan; Lovecraft, the recluse; [August] Derleth, the descendant of a count who fled the French revolution; [Seabury] Quinn and his interesting job." Bloch does not give an indication which of Quinn's jobs he has in mind, but he is perhaps referring to the fact that Quinn edited an undertakers' journal. See Robert Bloch, "About Our Authors," Weird Tales, September 1934, 396.

[169] H. P. Lovecraft, *Selected Letters 1929–1931*, ed. August Derleth and Donald Wandrei (Sauk City, WI: Arkham House, 1971), 371.

is fundamentally blind and corrupt, masking with rationality and prosaic indifference the reality that only a few outsiders can perceive. Just as their creators saw themselves as social outsiders, these characters frequently tread paths beyond the well-worn roads of society. While their writers chafed against the perceived unfairness of the dominant aesthetic that marginalized their art, these characters live in a cosmically unbalanced world, threatened by vast forces beyond their ability to control or even fully comprehend.[170] They stand alone against the forces of both blind neglect on the part of their contemporaries and the cosmic danger of the unknown. Thus, the weird class positions its fictive self-representation as sole possessors of genuine knowledge about the world, who, despite their privileged understanding, walk outside of society, seeing too much to integrate with a culture that does not understand them.[171]

In this study, I will examine how the weird class was constructed and how the outsider with access to true knowledge is represented both among the writers—and, to a lesser extent, their readers[172]—as well as their literary creations. First, I will examine the birth and evolution of *Weird Tales*, looking both at the creator's and editors' intentions for it and at the ongoing debate in the letter column about the literary status of the magazine. Next, I will consider how the genre of weird fiction helped shape the oppositional outsider rhetoric found in many of the stories of the magazine. I will then use Lovecraft's essay "Supernatural Horror in Literature" and his short story "The Unnamable" to demonstrate the way he positioned the ability to enjoy and create an uncanny effect as proof of superior aesthetic tastes and talent. I will then show how these ideas are also reflected in the writings of Robert E. Howard, another member of the Lovecraft Circle in whose stories the same themes take significantly different forms.

I choose the expression "weird class" to refer to the imagined set of writers and readers who are "sensitive" enough, to use Lovecraft's favored term, to appreciate weird literature. I do this to draw special attention to the class boundaries of that culture. Due to their own outsider status in society

---

[170] Carney writes about this cosmology of horror thus: "To the extent that it simulates a world deconstructing, a reality principle violated, it is an acutely 'agnostic' project with a thesis to impart, captured succinctly in an entry of Clark Ashton Smith's Black Book: 'All human thought, all science, all religion, is the holding of a candle to the night of the universe.'" Carney, "Shadow Modernism," 19.

[171] It should be noted, of course, that not all stories in *Weird Tales* match this formula, nor do even all stories written by the Lovecraft Circle; however, the pattern is pervasive and critical, and provides a fascinating insight into the mind-sets of these authors.

[172] As the rich correspondence through letters, "The Eyrie," and fan publications such as *Fantasy Fan* show, the readers of Weird Tales were deeply involved with the creation of the magazine and invested in the genre. The line between writer and reader was often crossed, with many writers expressing admiration for others' work and longtime readers trying their hand at producing their own weird stories and poems.

in general as well as the cultural marginalization of their chosen medium, this group both cuts across class boundaries and sets itself up oppositionally to the privileged class of writers who did not have to write for the proverbial penny per word to make a living. They belonged to writers of a new class: artists who had to write for a living.

This is not to say that the writers of the Lovecraft Circle all saw themselves as kindred to the pulp authors who pounded out formulaic story after story to meet the demands of the ravenous readership of magazines such as Black Mask and Argosy. It must be noted that Weird Tales was started to create a venue for publishing fiction that could not be found elsewhere rather than to milk profit from a popular theme. At this point, it was the weird story, not the pulp form, that marked the magazine as a place for a unique culture to flourish in the form of freedom of expression. Outsiderness was embedded in the magazine from the start. In the words of its founder, Jacob Clark Henneberger, the magazine's purpose was "to give the writer free rein to express his innermost feelings in a manner befitting great literature."[173] In 1923, when the magazine was founded, the common stereotypes about the shoddy quality of writing in the pulp magazines had not yet evolved. Henneberger could not have known that his chosen publication medium would lead to the magazine being associated with "the pulps."

In his dissertation, "The Shadow Modernism of Weird Tales: Experimental Pulp Fiction in the Age of Modernist Reflection," Jason Carney demonstrates a shift in the public perception of pulps, writing that "'pulp magazines' as a discrete 'Grub street' endeavor generalizable in terms of high quantity and low quality only became at hand as a circulating cultural stereotype after and as a result of the massive expansion of the all-fiction magazine marker."[174] Carney stresses that it was precisely as a means to create a new place for the publication of unique stories that had no other outlet that *Weird Tales* came about: "*Weird Tales* was founded in response to what the publisher, Jacob Clark Henneberger, thought of as an aesthetic crisis, a kind of encroachment of the contaminating commercial influence on literary endeavor."[175] Thus, it can be said that *Weird Tales*, at least at its inception, was not yet marked by the stamp of class marginalization that would later fall on the pulp form.[176] On the other hand, the genre of the weird story was

---

[173] Robert Weinberg, *The "Weird Tales" Story* (Rockville, MD: Borgo Press, 1999), 3.

[174] Carney, "Shadow Modernism," 35.

[175] Ibid., 35–36.

[176] Carney rejects the idea that *Weird Tales* preferred commercial interests over quality. He describes the magazine as "a non-commercial and aesthetically experimental enterprise informed by a desire to be a carnivalesque playground for otherwise uncategorizable and unsaleable manuscripts" that "challenges the notion that these magazines . . . were not concerned with issues of 'art' or entertain ideas of aesthetic ambition." Ibid., 41.

distinctly an outsider genre, as the lack of other publications that led to *Weird Tales's* creation illustrates.

As I mentioned, *Weird Tales* found itself increasingly associated with the general character of pulp magazines, which, "as a form, became the bottom of the cultural hierarchy of the 1920s and 1930s," according to David M. Earle, author of *Re-covering Modernism: Pulps, Paperbacks, and the Prejudice of Form.*[177] Even those responsible for the decisions made by *Weird Tales* had to struggle both to create quality work and to draw an audience to help the magazine stay afloat. Earle describes the balance pulp publishers had to strike when constructing their audience. On the one hand, they sought to appeal to readers from more privileged classes; on the other hand, they had to continue to sell to their core, working-class audience. The resulting discourse was complex and not easily summarized:

> These contemporary portraits of the pulp audience are complex—many selfdescriptive pulp editorials show a hopeful upward mobility, yet are careful not to ostracize the main, working-class readership. . . . For example, in 1935, A. A. Wyn wrote: "We all know that plenty of the bankers and brokers, lawyers and doctors, salesmen and Senators are addicted to reading the pulps."[178]

As writers of both weird fiction and a pulp magazine, the Lovecraft Circle was doubly marked by outsider status through the magazine's position in the broader world of literature. This anxiety was heightened by what some saw as pandering to scandalous interests. To attract more attention, *Weird Tales* often sported lurid covers depicting scantily clad women. The lively debate on this topic within the magazine's letter section, "The Eyrie," demonstrates the mixed feelings of the readers and writers regarding whether the magazine should aspire to literary status. Some readers felt scandalized by covers they said undermined the esteemed quality of the work in *Weird Tales*. In the August–September 1936 issue, Marshall Lemer of New York City, in a letter Farnsworth Wright titled "Is This Sarcasm?" writes,

> I admire the artistic sense that prompts Brundage to select invariably what is frequently the one nude in the entire issue for the cover illustration. . . . I receive a curious glance from the gentleman that presides over the local news stand when I ask for Weird Tales, and once I received a copy of Spice and Ginger Stories in pardonable error.[179]

---

[177] David M. Earle, *Re-covering Modernism: Pulps, Paperbacks, and the Prejudice of Form* (Farnham, UK: Ashgate, 1998), 36.

[178] Ibid., 87.

[179] Marshal Lemer, "Is This Sarcasm?," *Weird Tales*, August–September 1936, 252–53.

Other readers praised the covers for their artistry. In February 1938, Gertrude Hemken from Chicago, whose outspoken letters written in strong dialect were a regular staple of "The Eyrie," writes, "Wotta nude . . . ! Honestly, she looks almost real."[180] Wright, who took over from Edwin Baird as editor with *Weird Tales* in financial straits in 1924, took a pragmatic approach: the shocking covers sold magazines. Sometimes he took a similar approach to stories: "He featured stories many times that were not up to the quality of the other fiction in the magazine but which he knew would sell copies."[181] Thus, the magazine walked a line—one that would continue to be debated—between marketability and literary aspiration.

In terms of content, Wright included stories by famous authors of literary merit in his "Weird Reprints" section, further demonstrating the magazine's literary aspirations. Some of these writers included Charles Dickens, Jules Verne, Guy de Maupassant, and Edgar Allan Poe. Rather than attempting to elevate their favorites to join the ranks of accepted literary authors, enthusiasts of weird fiction situated their preferred form in terms of an alternate and equally valid literary tradition, one parallel to the widely accepted canon. To do so, they created their own means by which to judge the value of work, separate from the language of contemporary criticism. The conversation in "The Eyrie" richly praises and criticizes the stories of previous issues, using language suggestive of a set weird aesthetic, such as one letter from B. M. Reynolds in 1934: "Its cosmic scope and imaginative brilliance certainly give one food for thought."[182] And of another story, "If he can sustain the present high mark of eery mystery and nameless horror . . . , he will have written a masterpiece." Tone, imagination, and style are key to the weird aesthetic. Among phrases used by other contributors in that issue are such statements of aesthetic value as "sheer pathos and beauty," "unusual and original," "fantastic and imaginative," and "as good a piece of weird fiction as it is possible to find." The last sentence is worth particular note. Criticism is almost exclusively situated in this alternative aesthetic, rather than in terms of literature as a whole. The proponents of the weird tale made their claims to the merit of their chosen art form on their own terms.

Readers and writers alike judged the stories of Weird Tales in their own aesthetic terms, generally avoiding using the language of mainstream literature in their criticism. They often contextualized their praise with phrases such as "in the weird tales genre" and compared successful writers to others who wrote in that mode. I chose the October 1937 issue to examine the letter column for comparisons of the work that appeared in the magazine to other literature. There are five instances of *Weird Tales* writers being

---

[180] Gertrude Hemken, "Trudy Answers Our Critics," *Weird Tales*, August–September 1936, 252.
[181] Weinberg, *"Weird Tales" Story*, 31.
[182] B. M. Reynolds, "A New High Mark," *Weird Tales*, September 1934, 394.

compared to other writers of the weird who did not appear in the magazine except in the reprints, notably Poe and H. G. Wells. These comparisons are all positive, illustrating the readers' interest in connecting their favorites to the more acceptable stories of previous generations. In this way, they helped solidify the pedigree and ongoing continuity of the literary respectability of their genre. Interestingly, writers are only compared to other Weird Tales writers three times. No writers in the magazine are likened to contemporary writers who did not write weird fiction.

The only other writer mentioned is Hemingway, and the mention uses Hemingway as the opposite of weird writers. That particular letter warrants special attention, as Wright chose it to lead the column and dedicated almost a page and a half to its content and his own rebuttal of it. It provides a fascinating insight into the balance between popular entertainment and literature that the magazine sought. The letter writer, G. M. Wilson, complains that the virtuous characters in the magazine inevitably win. He could not have won favor with Wright by his choice of wording: "I read some years ago that a writer who wished to achieve success with *your type* of magazine must never let heroism be overcome by villainy"[183] (emphasis mine). He anticipates that Wright might give a typical reply about not aspiring to a realistic, and hence not literary, representation of life, but insists that *Weird Tales* is not a typical pulp: "You may say you are not writing about life, that I can get my sordid realism in the contemporary fiction of the Hemingway school, but . . . [t]he point is that you have the makings of an excellent magazine, above the class of the usual pulp, yet you usually and deliberately tie yourself down with this one flaw"[184] (emphasis mine).

Wright might well have taken special umbrage at the tone taken by Wilson, which places his argument in commercial terms and suggests that the editorial choices taken by the staff are purely to please readers and sell the maximum number of copies: "I suppose you are a success financially and have a large reading public, but don't you think you could widen your appeal and increase circulation by adopting the above suggestion? . . . [I]t is your business to know the psychology of your reading public."[185] Wilson's assumptions, as we have seen, were basically wrong; *Weird Tales* was not doing well, and perhaps was never meant to. In the response he felt compelled to write, Wright makes clear his dedication to quality weird literature over

---

[183] G. M. Wilson, "Does Virtue Always Win?," *Weird Tales*, October 1937, 503.

[184] Ibid., 504.

[185] Ibid. Though it indicates that Wilson separated *Weird Tales* from pulp literature in his mind, it is ironic that he encourages Wright to do exactly the opposite of what more successful pulp magazines were doing: he tells Wright to make his stories less formulaic and predictable in order to sell more copies. In doing so, he imagines an audience that wants the opposite of what pulp audiences were commonly thought to want: generic stories repeated issue after issue in which the end is never in doubt.

predictable potboilers. He describes two stories that caused particular outrage from readers for violent fates that befell their characters, and he names four stories in just the previous issue in which virtue does not triumph. "Most[186] of our stories do end happily because that is the way the authors write them; but our readers can never know in advance whether the ending will be happy or otherwise."[187]

Agreeing with Wright, Weinberg argues that the unpredictable nature of weird fiction allowed writers to push their imaginings even beyond those of other magazines, setting their stories in other worlds, which were often thinly veiled analogues of the contemporary world. "The one thing readers knew with *Weird Tales* was that the unexpected was always possible. For if the reader knew in advance that the ending would always be a happy one, then all threats and occurrences in the tale could not dispel the knowledge that all would be well in the end. . . . It was that extra dimension that gave *Weird Tales* the monopoly on real horror stories during the era."[188] The defamiliarizing[189] influence of the weird tale allowed writers to reshape the contemporary world and make it new in the eyes of the readers. This allowed writers broader freedom to criticize elements of society and to promote their own worldviews; one can see the realworld analogues behind the cosmic horrors, barbarians, and aliens between the covers of Weird Tales.

This defamiliarizing effect is particularly strong in this genre of fiction and explains why *Weird Tales* could function so effectively in its construction of its own class identity. According to Istvan Csicsery-Ronay Jr. in The Seven Beauties of Science Fiction, science fiction provides a sense of wonder in two primary modes: the sublime and the grotesque. These he defines, respectively, as "a complex recoil and recuperation of self-consciousness coping with phenomena suddenly perceived to be too great to be

---

[186] In the December 1937 issue, Clifton Hall writes in to address Wilson's letter. Hall writes that he "checked back over the stories—exactly 90 of them, including reprints—that have appeared in the ten issues dated 1937, and found out a surprising fact. There was an exact split—45–45—between the happy and unhappy endings!" He admits that "it was difficult to definitely place many yarns in either classification," but insists that this ratio shows "an amazing balance of endings." Clifton Hall, "Happy vs. Unhappy Endings," *Weird Tales*, December 1937, 765.

[187] Farnsworth Wright, untitled introduction to "The Eyrie," *Weird Tales*, October 1937, 503.

[188] Weinberg, *"Weird Tales" Story*, 33–34.

[189] Here I rely on Shklovsky's definition of defamiliarization: "Art exists that one may recover the sensation of life; it exists to make one feel things, to make the stone stony. The purpose of art is to impart the sensation of things as they are perceived and not as they are known. The technique of art is to make objects "unfamiliar," to make forms difficult, to increase the difficulty and length of perception because the process of perception is an aesthetic end in itself and must be prolonged." See Viktor Shklovsky, "Art as Technique," in *Literary Theory: An Anthology*, ed. Julie Rivkin and Michael Ryan, 2nd ed. (Maiden, MA: Blackwell Publishing, 2004), 16.

comprehended" and "the realization that objects that appear to be familiar . . . are actually undergoing surprising transformations."[190] It is clear that weird fiction falls into both categories. These stories serve to destabilize the audience's beliefs in rigid concepts: "In both, the perceiver enjoys a sudden dislocation from habitual perception" in which "the testing of the categories conventionally used to interpret the world, and the desire to articulate what consciousness finds inarticulable."[191] "Behind all of the specific moments are vast and vastly changed conceptual vistas that make possible new imaginary experiences and ways of inhabiting material existence."[192] It is precisely such "vastly changed conceptual vistas" that the weird class inhabited. The writers of the Lovecraft Circle did more than write for pay: they used their imaginative output to produce a new and alternative literary society that reshaped preconceptions about art and the lived experience of artists.

## "SUPERNATURAL HORROR IN LITERATURE"

Lovecraft explicitly explains his perception of the relationship of weird fiction to literature at large in "Supernatural Horror in Literature," in which he also lays out his ideas arguing for the superiority of his chosen genre, and therefore the writers of it. In the essay, he creates a dichotomy between the imagination of the weird story[193] and the banality of other literature, yet he also presents weird literature as the principal means of conveying horror, as much a part of human experience as any other emotion captured by other writers. Thus, he presents weird fiction as both more imaginative than and as emotionally true as contemporary literature.

In his essay, he suggests that those who dedicate themselves to stories about mundane events lack imagination: "Relatively few are free enough from the spell of the daily routine to respond to rappings from outside, and tales of ordinary feelings and events, or of common sentimental distortions of such feelings and events, will always take first place in the taste of the majority."[194] In the language he uses, such as the expression "free from the

---

[190] Istvan Csicsery-Ronay Jr., *The Seven Beauties of Science Fiction* (Middletown, CT: Wesleyan University Press, 2008), 146.

[191] Ibid., 147.

[192] Ibid., 148.

[193] Lovecraft defines "the true weird tale" thus: "The true weird tale has something more than secret murder, bloody bones, or a sheeted form clanking chains according to rule. A certain atmosphere of breathless and unexplainable dread of outer, unknown forces must be present; and there must be a hint, expressed with a seriousness and portentousness becoming its subject, of that most terrible conception of the human brain—a malign and particular suspension or defeat of those fixed laws of Nature which are our only safeguard against the assaults of chaos and the daemons of unplumbed space." H. P. Lovecraft, "Supernatural Horror in Literature," in *At the Mountains of Madness: The Definitive Edition* (New York: Modern Library, 2005), 105.

[194] Ibid.

spell," we see his preferencing of the supernatural over the mundane, which he positioned as deadening to the ability to perceive true beauty. Those who write and enjoy weird stories are not bound by the "common" and "ordinary." Lovecraft specifically attributes inability to appreciate weird fiction to a lack of sensitivity and insists that the ability to enjoy supernatural horror exists only among a select elite: "But the sensitive are always with us . . . ; so that no amount of rationalization, reform, or Freudian analysis can quite annul the thrill of the chimney-corner whisper or the lonely wood." It is worth noting that he places rationalism and modernity (to use his word, "reform") as opponents of his chosen genre. He insists that his "tradition" is "as real and as deeply grounded in mental experience as any other pattern or tradition of mankind," thus claiming that supernatural horror is as capable of representing human reality as other forms of literature. In doing so, Lovecraft does something many of his contemporaries do not: he favorably compares weird literature to mainstream fiction in terms of craft and representation rather than merely content.[195]

As is usual to the writers and readers of weird fiction, Lovecraft establishes a system for assessing quality within the genre itself, comparing weird stories only to other weird stories when he describes the qualities that mark a particularly successful piece: "If the proper sensations are excited, such a 'high spot' must be admitted *on its own merits* as weird literature" (emphasis mine). He also takes pains to separate his favored literary form from that which might too easily be dismissed as being hackneyed or trashy: "The true weird tale has something more than secret murder, bloody bones, or a sheeted form clanking chains according to rule."[196] Lovecraft, who believed he had been born in the wrong century, fit perfectly into the outsiders of the weird class brought together by *Weird Tales*. What for his characters is a source of terror and often mental and physical harm was a source of some hope for Lovecraft: that his artistic endeavors showed his greater sensitivity toward a unique and vibrant art form. It also revealed a duality to his relationship with the literary elite: he presented their unwillingness to accept his art form as an inability to appreciate it.

# H. P. LOVECRAFT

Lovecraft's class consciousness was specifically formed by his sense of having fallen from a superior station. From boyhood, Howard Phillips Lovecraft was made aware of his family's reduced financial and social status, and his chosen career as a writer of weird stories further strained his position. Lovecraft was born "to a family that was both well-to-do financially and a part of the

---

[195] Ibid.
[196] Ibid.

informal social aristocracy of" Providence, Rhode Island.[197] His father died a gruesome death in 1898 of what is now believed to be syphilis. In 1904, when Lovecraft was fourteen, the mismanagement of his grandfather's estate "forced the family to move . . . into a smaller house."[198] Deeply shamed, he later wrote of himself in this time, "How could an old man of 14 . . . readjust his existence to a skimpy flat and new household programme and inferior outdoor setting . . . ?" and contemplated suicide.[199] His desire to escape his current circumstances surfaced frequently in life and found its expression through his writing; he later wrote, "There is no field other than the weird in which I have any aptitude or inclination for fictional composition. Life has never interested me so much as the escape from life."[200] Never having attended university, Lovecraft felt the shame of his academic failure all his life. In his construction of cosmic forces in his stories, he separates access not only to imagination but also to knowledge from the privileged academic class.

In many of Lovecraft's stories, true horror comes not from physical danger, but from the realization that the universe is fundamentally ambivalent toward humanity. By making contact with forces that bring irrefutable knowledge about the inhuman nature of the cosmos, Lovecraft's characters cross from a place of ignorance to one of understanding. Their understanding of the very places with which they were most familiar, which they imagined to be complete and fixed, becomes unhinged as they see the fundamental disharmony of the universe. James Kneale demonstrates that, for someone with Lovecraft's conservative perspectives on change and space, the liminal divisions between imagined worlds where such contact is possible become a site of anxiety. He writes that, "while thresholds can be read positively or negatively, Lovecraft usually casts his in a negative light because they open up the prospect of change, which can only be threatening to someone obsessed with fixity."[201]

In his story "The Unnamable," Lovecraft challenges what he sees as a bourgeois prejudice against weird stories, which he attributes to a failure of imagination. In the story, Lovecraft presents an argument between the narrator and his friend, who represents a straw man for contemporary literature. Their debate, which begins about art, moves into basic questions about the essential nature of reality: Whose knowledge of the realities of the world is more complete?

---

197 H. P. Lovecraft, *Lord of a Visible World: An Autobiography in Letters*, ed. S. T. Joshi and David E. Schultz (Athens: Ohio University Press, 2000), 8.

198 Ibid., 9.

199 Ibid., 30.

200 Ibid., 270.

201 James Kneale, "From Beyond: H. P. Lovecraft and the Place of Horror," *Cultural Geographies* 13, no. 1 (2006): 120.

The narrator tries to convince Joel Manton, "an orthodox sun-dweller" whose "feelings had fixed dimensions, properties, causes, and effects," of the "mystical and unexplained."[202] As Lovecraft's narrator insists, "'Common sense' in reflecting on these subjects . . . is merely a stupid absence of imagination and mental flexibility." Again, Lovecraft emphasizes the importance of sensitivity to things not felt by most: "No wonder sensitive students shudder at the Puritan age in Massachusetts."[203]

Lovecraft's satire of contemporary literature is clear in his description of the literary preferences of Manton, for whom anything imaginative is anathema, and the most thorough examination of banal everyday events constitutes true art: It was his view that only our normal, objective experiences possess any esthetic significance, and that it is the province of the artist not so much to rouse strong emotion by action, ecstasy, and astonishment, as to maintain a placid interest and appreciation by accurate, detailed transcripts of everyday affairs.

> Especially did he object to my preoccupation with the mystical and the unexplained;
> or although believing in the supernatural much more fully than I, he
> would not admit that it is sufficiently commonplace for literary treatment.[204]

After the inevitable confrontation with the horror that proves the narrator's fears, the narrator is left "too dazed to exult."[205] In this moment, Lovecraft's own hope for the triumph of the uncanny over rationality, and therein the triumph of Lovecraft's form of mystical knowledge over accepted academia, is clear. Though the narrator is almost destroyed by the experience, his understanding of the universe is definitively proven.[206]

For Lovecraft, who aspired to the identity of a scholar despite his inability to enter academia, the world of politics and science felt as distant and apathetic as the gods of his stories. For all his class pretensions due to his heritage, Lovecraft's poverty was a constant reminder of this outsider status.

---

202 H. P. Lovecraft, "The Unnamable," in *The Dreams in the Witch House and Other Weird Stories*, ed. S. T. Joshi (New York: Penguin Classics, 2004), 83.

203 Ibid., 85.

204 Ibid., 83.

205 Ibid., 89.

206 It may be worth mentioning what probably goes without saying: that this proof is hardly ever comforting to the characters who come to it, but is rather deeply disturbing, as it reveals a universe fundamentally corrupt and out of balance. In this case, vindication and relief are polar opposites: those who live in ignorance are the happy ones. Thus, those who may be imagined to be in the comfortable bosom of the literary elite are positioned as happy, while those outsiders whose comfort is their art and their peers in the "weird class" must contend with the burden of fundamental anxieties about the disturbed order of things—an order that leaves them on the margins of the literary world. For all their success in the pages of *Weird Tales*, writers like Lovecraft never enjoyed acceptance into mainstream literature.

He writes of his frustration that his stories did not achieve broader acceptance among readers, and he chafed at the public perception of "the pulps." As such, many of Lovecraft's stories form tacit arguments that there is a vital science beyond academic knowledge, which is the knowledge of the uncanny and unknowable that his stories seek to capture.[207] However, for all his imagination and understanding, Lovecraft still saw himself as spurned by the literary elite.

Just as Lovecraft's anxieties about his relationship with accepted society were expressed in his stories, so was his terror of the lower class—a class he refused to imagine he himself had become part of, despite the dire financial straits that necessitated his ghostwriting for other authors to earn his meager living. The volume of his outfit was barely enough for him to get by. After he married Sonia Haft Greene, an immigrant of Ukrainian and Jewish descent,[208] he moved to New York City, where his finances forced him to take residence in Brooklyn. There, he lived elbow to elbow with uneducated, often foreign-born people. For Lovecraft, the idea that he, a "sensitive" member of the weird class, could belong among such people was a source of terrible loathing. His class disgust is strongly tinged with xenophobia, and in his letters he attributes the decay of that part of the city to the influence of immigrants: "My guess is that its decay had just set in, owing to the Syrian fringe beyond Atlantic Avenue."[209] After he finally leaves New York, he writes, "It is nearly a full year ago that I left it without a pang to come home to my own—to the clean, white, and ancient New England that bred me."[210] By returning to New England, he believed he came closer to the proper balance owed to one of his ancient family and artistic abilities, though he would never achieve the affluence and success he felt was his birthright.

Lovecraft's deep feelings of outsiderness driven home by his stay in Brooklyn appear in an infamous story he wrote based on this experience, "The Horror at Red Hook." The story, which Lovecraft's wife later suggested was born from a rude encounter with a group of workers at a restaurant, connects the tendency toward laziness, criminality, and vice that Lovecraft

---

[207] In one of Lovecraft's few weird stories that may be said to have a triumphant ending, "The Dunwich Horror," the abomination from beyond the realm of human understanding is destroyed by the faculty of the fictional Miskatonic University. This university is worth special mention, as it is both a respected academic institution and a place of weird knowledge. It has, for example, in its collection a copy of the famous Necronomicon. While the faculty members who study occult phenomena are shunned by their peers even at Miskatonic, their theories prove to be founded in bitter reality. Thus, Lovecraft imagines other "aged academics" whose interest in strange sciences mirrors his own and who have achieved at least marginal acceptance in academia.

[208] Lovecraft, *Lord of a Visible World*, xiii.

[209] Ibid., 164.

[210] Ibid., 167.

saw in his neighbors with another fear—that of ancient, pagan, blasphemous rites threatening the city.

In the story, the slum Red Hook, once a respectable neighborhood, is now multiracial, occupied by "Syrian, Spanish, Italian, and negro elements."[211] By constructing the menace of the neighborhood thus, Lovecraft exerted artistic domination over his class environment by recasting his anxiety in terms of the cosmic horrors of his own imagination. Thus, he imagined a bizarre and unknown "truth" literally lurking beneath the thing he despised. This fictional Red Hook is "a babel of sound and filth, and sends out strange cries to answer the lapping of oily waves at its grimy piers."[212] "From this tangle of material and spiritual putrescence the blasphemies of an hundred dialects assail the sky. Hordes of prowlers reel shouting and singing along the lanes . . . and swarthy, sin-pitted faces disappear from windows when visitors pick their way through."[213] This depraved, destitute population worships evil pre-Christian gods and kidnaps innocents for sacrifice to their gods. "Here cosmic sin had entered, and festered by unhallowed rites had commenced the grinning march of death that was to rot us all to fungous abnormalities too hideous for the grave's holding."[214]

The story thus creates a bizarre conjunction: the illiterate immigrant masses worship eldritch beings of secret power. It must be noted, however, that the immigrants make sacrifices to something they do not understand, which is corrupting New York and America from the inside. This "rotting," literal in the story, reflects the metaphorical social rot Lovecraft feared coming from the multiracial lower class. At its heart, this xenophobia fears the loss of the privilege claimed by whiteness, a fear embodied by miscegenation. Even the idea that the supposedly superior white race would or even could be combined with other races and thus lose their distinction threatens to remove the distinction itself, exposing the fragility of the ideology of white supremacy. At the climax of the story, the detective Malone discovers "solitary prisoners in a state of complete idiocy . . . including four mothers with infants of disturbingly strange appearance. These infants died soon after exposure to light; a circumstance the doctors thought rather merciful."[215] This discovery illuminates the horror that the lower classes will literally bring forth abomination. In this case, the forced mating of humans with monsters closely mirrors Lovecraft's phobia of the intermingling of classes and races.

The terrors of the secret world here threaten to spill over into the familiar, sun-drenched New York its dwellers thought they understood. Malone, as a

---

[211] H. P. Lovecraft, "The Horror at Red Hook," in *Dreams in the Witch House*, 119.
[212] Ibid.
[213] Ibid., 120.
[214] Ibid., 132.
[215] Ibid., 135.

white man, glimpses a reality that shakes his worldview to the core: a world in which the human, white or otherwise, is not a privileged creature, and whiteness signifies no distinction. This remains a mystery to the others, who are unable to grasp its portents: "Malone thinks these detectives shew a sadly limited perspective in their lack of wonder at the myriad unexplainable details." In an interesting turn, Malone wishes the things he experienced in real life could again be confined to mere fantasy, a story such as one the readers of Weird Tales might enjoy: "But he is content to rest silent in Chepachet [a small town in Rhode Island], calming his nervous system and praying that time may gradually transfer his terrible experience from the realm of present reality to that of picturesque and semimythical remoteness."[216] This connection back to the enjoyment of distant fantasy seems to raise the question how the assumed white reader of the story might respond to its destabilization of race and class. One might assume, based on Malone's experience, that this reaction was imagined to be similar horror based in deeply racist and classist attitudes.

Though the fundamental disordering of the universe extends to the upper class in "The Horror at Red Hook," the story betrays Lovecraft's fondness for the privileged old world. One character, Robert Suydam, is characteristic of Lovecraft's representations of the upper class, a decadent scion who serves as a reminder of a better age. In the mold of Roderick Usher, whose "time-honored" family "had put forth, at no period, any enduring branch,"[217] Suydam is "a lettered recluse of an ancient Dutch family . . . inhabiting the spacious but ill-preserved mansion which his grandfather had built."[218]

Though he, too, is destroyed, Suydam does strike back in death at the unholy force that slew him. After Suydam falls under the corrupting influence of Red Hook's witchcraft and dies, his "naked, tittering, phosphorescent" corpse pushes the cursed idol from its a pedestal in its underground lair, freeing the community—although temporarily—from the power of that inhuman god. In Suydam's character, the reader finds a combination of the decayed and fallen aristocracy of Poe with this final moment of posthumous redemption. Though he himself is as dead as the era in which his family was still ascendant, Suydam fights at the chaotic disorder of the universe. The fondness for the old aristocracy lingers in Lovecraft's story, even with the passing of the last of that ancient family.

Lovecraft's writing shows a deep fear that social imbalances would lead to the complete destruction of civilization, which he saw as already fallen from its height at the eighteenth century ideal. Paul Buhle argues, "In asociality and in history, Horror is the natural concomitant to the Socialist

---

[216] Ibid., 137.

[217] Edgar Allan Poe, *Poetry, Tales, and Selected Essays* (New York: Library of America, 1996), 318.

[218] Lovecraft, "The Horror at Red Hook," 121.

critiques of Capitalism. Horror foreshadows and fulfils the Marxian prediction of Socialism or Barbarism by placing in true perspective the breakdown of the West."[219] At the base of Lovecraft's fiction is the fundamental challenge of modern science on the established order. If the evolution of humans is a natural process without inherent meaning, there arises what Buhle calls "a modern sense of indeterminacy."[220] This creates a sense of meaninglessness and hopelessness that ever threatens to crush the sanity of Lovecraft's characters; the cosmic horrors of his stories signify the vast ambivalence of the flawed universe.

For Lovecraft, his own loss of familial prestige, coupled with the humiliation of his reduced circumstances and of his being forced to rely on his writing to survive, created a terrible sense of helplessness and inconsequentiality. He saw himself ostracized from both academia and the greater literary world, and he imagined himself separate from both, creating his own artistic circle with the other writers and the readers of the magazines for which he wrote. In his stories, this disordered balance almost always leads to ruin for the characters who realize it.

## ROBERT E. HOWARD

The lone outsider who comes into possession of secret knowledge about the fundamentally flawed universe also appears in the work of Robert E. Howard. For Howard, this corruption did not come from a fall from grace with the close of a previous era, but rather from a fundamental flaw in civilization itself. Like Lovecraft's, Howard's characters frequently discover, to their horror, that the illusion of normalcy in the world is a thin skin stretched over a maddeningly vast truth. There is far more to the world than most imagine, and that which we call civilization is guided by sinister forces incomprehensible to most. Unlike Lovecraft's characters, Howard's heroes frequently rise to fight back against the terrors of the cosmic night, though their victory is a fleeting one: the corruption, ultimately, is insurmountable.

Born in a small Texas town in 1906, Howard witnessed as a young man the transition from frontier life to a modern small town. Howard saw the effects the wealth of an oil boom has on a region. He wrote, "Oil came into the country when I was still a young boy, and remained. I'll say one thing about an oil boom; it will teach a kid that Life's a pretty rotten thing about as quick as anything I can think of."[221] As Mark Finn writes in his biography of

---

[219] Paul Buhle, "Dystopia as Utopia: Howard Phillips Lovecraft and the Unknown Content of American Horror Literature," in *H. P. Lovecraft: Four Decades of Criticism*, ed. S. T. Joshi (Athens: Ohio University Press, 1980), 219.

[220] Ibid., 203.

[221] Leon Nielson, *Robert E. Howard: A Collector's Descriptive Bibliography of American and British Hardcover, Paperback, Magazine, Special and Amateur Editions, with a Biography* (London: McFarland, 2007).

Howard, *Blood and Thunder*, "Robert's reaction formed a moral stance that he would strike over and over again in the wood pulp pages of Weird Tales magazine and its many competitors. A sensitive man, who felt deeply, he couldn't help but be affected by the constant chaos, violence, and corruption that came with the oil booms."[222] Howard was something of a contradiction, an amateur boxer as well as a voracious reader and writer. The people of his small town did not understand him, and Howard chafed at their perception of him, though he did have a circle of close friends and correspondents. He, like Lovecraft and other members of their circle, lived on the fringe of normal society.

Howard's stories echo Lovecraft's in that the outsider protagonists' ability to access forbidden knowledge sets them apart from their society and gives them power. Like Lovecraft's heroes, Howardian characters are often placed in peril by their exposure to dangers on the borders of the rational world. Just as Lovecraft's horrors crept into the minds of those sensitive enough to glimpse them, the danger of the peek into forbidden truth frequently challenges Howard's characters. Howard's protagonists, in contrast to Lovecraft's academics, are true working-class heroes. They exemplify virtues of rough masculinity, physical strength, combat prowess, hard work, toughness, and courage. Often, the protagonist can be identified as soon as a broad-chested, thick-armed, battle-ready character appears. They have other things in common with Lovecraft's characters: they are social outsiders, they struggle with forces partially beyond their comprehension, and they are prone to brooding reflections on the mysteries of the universe. Most of all, they stand alone.

That Howard hated the idea of working for others is well documented. In a 1931 letter to Farnsworth Wright, Howard wrote, "Life's not worth living if somebody thinks he's in authority over you."[223] Writing was an opportunity to be his own master, and Howard chafed at social conventions. Even Howard's barbarian heroes appear apart from their tribes and places of origin, traveling alone and out of place in a wider world. While their harsh upbringings have hardened them to survive in the violent worlds Howard describes, these heroes are separated from membership in any larger group. They wander, often alone and at odds with the powers that control their world. Their success or failure depends on their ability to assert their individualism and control their own fate. Wealth translates to the power to exert one's will, often as a corollary to masculine assertion of violence. This is not a gesture of domination of others, but rather of securing one's individual freedom. As it did with Lovecraft, writing gave Howard a chance to control his own destiny in a fundamentally flawed world.

---

[222] Mark Finn, *Blood and Thunder: The Life and Art of Robert E. Howard* (Austin, TX: Monkeybrain, 2006), 17.

[223] Nielsen, *Robert E. Howard*, 17.

A recurring theme in Howard's works is the decadent civilization on the verge of collapse, particularly characterized by senseless warfare and sexual deviance. In his letters, he is ever against capitalistic greed and exploitation: he writes against the "gang that are now ham-stringing the administration and yelling 'Communism!' every time Roosevelt tries to free the country a little from their monopolistic clutches."[224] In his correspondence, he writes with great passion about barbarian cultures and the muscular freedom of the cowboys heroes whose last light was fading even then. He, like Lovecraft, believed the best age of the world had passed, though he placed this mantle on the broad shoulders of barbarians rather than the Romans and the eighteenth century English, as Lovecraft did.

The power and danger of forbidden knowledge about the universe reveal themselves with remarkable clarity in the stories of King Kull. Their treatment is particularly nuanced in "The Shadow Kingdom." Kull is himself a barbarian from the island of Atlantis, ruling in a time even before the rise of the advanced civilization now associated with that island. In Kull's age, the mighty state of Valusia rules the world, and he is its king. This position forces him to glimpse secrets not meant for humans: that power as he knows it is a lie and that humans, far from being lords of the planet, are merely pawns in a cosmic game they can little comprehend.

Kull receives his first warning about this from the Pictish ambassador Kanu, who is himself an outsider: as a Pict, he will never be entirely welcomed by the Valusians, but his long years as an ambassador have made him fat, too fond—by his own admission—of wine and women. His position outside both cultures gives him membership in the outsider weird class, and thus unique insight: he combines half-forgotten Pictish legends with what he knows of the secrets of Valusia's politics to glimpse the truth about the ancient history of Valusia's leadership, and so he warns Kull, "The night can hear. There are worlds within worlds."[225] His words begin to part the veil that hides the truth from Kull.

This warning weighs heavily on Kull, for whom the place of the city itself becomes suddenly strange and sinister. He perceives that order is only an illusion for something fundamentally alien to him, which both makes him an outsider and threatens him: "You and your tribe shall pass, but we are invincible, indestructible. We towered above a strange world, ere Atlantis and Lemuria rose from the sea."[226] This is the threat of a past in which the current divisions between reality and imagination were not so sharp, and humans

---

[224] H. P. Lovecraft and Robert E. Howard, *A Means to Freedom: The Letters of H. P. Lovecraft and Robert E. Howard*, ed. S. T. Joshi, David E. Schultz, and Rusty Burke (New York: Hippocampus Press, 2009), 89.

[225] Robert E. Howard, *Kull: Exile of Atlantis*, ed. Patrice Louinet (New York: Ballantine, 2006), 22.

[226] Ibid., 24.

fought to survive against things known only in legends.[227] Just as the city, with its rigid class hierarchies and its masses of unimaginative people who little know the truth about the place they live, was a source of anxiety in Lovecraft's work, it is alienating in Howard's stories as well.

Thus, as in the works of Lovecraft, the separation of the mundane world and illusion is disturbed by a terrifying truth: that those things sensitive people fear are real, waiting in constant menace just beyond the perception of most. Kull learns that the course of human history has been controlled by a race of evil serpent-people, who disguise themselves as human priests and kings. They conspire to kill and replace Kull with one of their own. As Kull creeps through his own palace, the familiar halls made strange by the new realization of the secrets within, he feels his perception of reality changing. He feels "like a naked child before the inscrutable wisdom of the mystic past. Again the sense of unreality swept upon him. At the back of his soul stole dim, gigantic phantoms, whispering monstrous things."[228]

The reader sees just how disordered the world has become for Kull as he perceives the hidden truth and grapples with the significance of this hidden knowledge: "[H]is flesh crawled with a horrid thought; 'are the people of Valusia men or are they *all* serpents?'"[229] (emphasis in original). As what he previously believed to exist only in myth proves to be real, Kull fights to reorient himself as to what is real and what is not. He suddenly questions everything he had previously taken for granted. Though this hesitation would leave the psyche of one of Lovecraft's characters crippled, Kull is made of stronger stuff, and he steels himself for a fight.

Tall and muscular, Kull little resembles a Lovecraftian protagonist, but his ability to sense—and even be terrified by—the reality of his world demonstrates that he, too, is a fictional representative of the weird class. As a king and a barbarian, he is doubly on the margins of society, ruling over a strange and ancient people he has no kinship with. In an interesting turn,

Kull's outsider imagination is able to glimpse what the common people of Valusia have themselves forgotten: the supernatural forces that peer from the recesses of the past and still lurk in the dark corners of the city.

The secret to his survival comes out of the dim past, together with the inhuman menace that threatens to overwhelm Kull.[230] Brule, a Pictish warrior sent by Ka-nu, reveals to Kull the ancient phrase "Ka nama kaa lajerama,"

---

[227] These are named to Kull later: "the bird-women, the harpies, the bat-men, the flying fiends, the wolf-people, the demons, the goblins." Ibid., 36.

[228] Ibid., 35.

[229] Ibid., 35.

[230] In many Howard stories, just as in many Lovecraft stories, modernity itself is portrayed as a thin and illusive mask stretched over reality. When this mask is pierced, one perceives a reality that was better known in the shadowy past, when humanity was steeped in occult wisdom and closer to the fundamental forces that move the cosmos. This opposition to and undermining of modernity is a key element in the work of both authors.

which humans can pronounce but serpent-men cannot, thus serving as a shibboleth. Kull, served both by the secret knowledge imparted to him by the Picts and by his own overwhelming physical prowess, defeats the serpentmen with the help of Brule. This, like many Howard stories, features the victory of an outsider character who walks beyond the borders of normal society and possesses knowledge that average humans do not have access to.

Much has been written about Howard's complex worldview regarding the struggle between civilization and barbarism, and it would be a disservice to suggest that he completely preferred the latter over the former. It is, however, clear that in civilization itself Howard found an element of the fundamental corruption of the world. In the battle between the snake-cult and those with knowledge of their presence, he stages the opposition between those forces that control humans who go through life little guessing the deeper truths hidden beyond their understanding:

> He stopped short, staring, for suddenly, like the silent swinging wide of a mystic door, misty, unfathomed reaches opened in the recesses of his consciousness and for an instant he seemed to gaze back through the vastnesses that spanned life and life; seeing through the vague and ghostly fogs dim shapes reliving dead centuries—men in combat with hideous monsters, vanquishing a planet of frightful terrors. . . . And man, the jest of the gods, the blind, wisdomless striver from dust to dust, following the long bloody trail of his destiny, knowing not why, bestial, blundering, like a great murderous child, yet feeling somewhere a spark of divine fire.[231]

In the next sentence, the reader sees a vital clue to Kull's own perception of the universe: "Kull drew a hand across his brow, shaken; these sudden glimpses into the abysses of memory always startled him." The phrasing "these sudden glimpses . . . always startled him" demonstrates that he is prone to these imaginings and has had them before; Kull, too, is sensitive[232] to the same cosmic secrets that Lovecraft's characters are. Rather than buckling to the pressures of what he knows, he rages against it, despite shuddering at the

---

[231] Howard, *Kull*, 36.

[232] It may seem at first glance that Howard's more famous creation, Conan, does not share this sensitivity, but this would be a mistake. Conan's philosophy does not deny that he understands that the world is controlled by secret and sinister forces beyond what most humans know; instead, he declares only that he does not wish to understand them. As he expresses in "Queen of the Black Coast": "I seek not beyond death. It may be the blackness averred by the Nemedian skeptics, or Crom's realm of ice and cloud, or the snowy plains and vaulted halls of the Nordheimer's Valhalla. I know not, nor do I care. Let me live deep while I live." In that story, he pays dearly for failing to open his imagination to the possibilities suggested by an ancient ruin, and in the end it is only by such a supernatural occurrence—one that, in addition, gives a suggestion to this earlier question of his—that Conan survives. See Robert E. Howard, "Queen of the Black Coast," in *The Coming of Conan the Cimmerian*, ed. Patrice Louinet (New York: Ballantine, 2003), 134.

realization of his own insignificant place in the cosmos. It is this sensitivity that makes him such a strong warrior against the mysteries the world hides, demonstrating his fitness both to rule and to be a worthy member of the weird class in literature.

## CONCLUSION

The aesthetic of the weird class took shape through their writings. Rather than through face-to-face interaction, the Lovecraft Circle expressed their ideas about their role as writers of weird stories on the fringes of literature through their stories, poems, and letters. Just as the character of the outsider who gains knowledge of the secret corruption of the universe that exists beyond the understanding of most appears in Lovecraft's and Howard's work, this same pattern can be found in the writings of other Lovecraft Circle authors. It can be traced through the bizarre imaginary worlds of Clark Ashton Smith, where individuals wander lost and amazed, acted upon by forces they little understand. It is found in C. L. Moore's stories about Jirel of Joiry and Northwest Smith, eternal wanderers on the edge of civilization whose every story is an encounter with the strange forces beyond the pale, one in the past and the other in the future. In the stories of what S. T. Joshi has termed the Lovecraft Mythos, written by such authors as Robert Bloch, Fritz Leiber, Frank Belknap Long, and Henry Kuttner, we see the use of elements of Lovecraft's cosmology: the sensitive protagonist who glimpses behind the veil that hides universal truths from the minds of most, the vast and sinister chaos of the world. The truths glimpsed or revealed reflect social and personal fears of the writers, often proving to be startling pictures of oppressive ideologies of race, sex, and class. This is not to say that these stories are cast from the same mold; every writer adds a unique turn to these themes, and there is space for exploration of the interplay of their themes with the influences of the weird class.

Each member of the Lovecraft Circle expressed ideas of alienation, of the triumph of the weird imagination, and of the fundamental wrongness of the universe that, when detected by those sensitive enough to perceive it, brings both understanding and madness. It is little wonder that, in the stories these writers tell, characters who express this weird imagination suffer for it more often than not, and ultimate destruction at the hands—or tentacles—of irresistible universal forces proves to be the fate of humanity regardless of the small victories the heroes might achieve. Pushed to the literary fringe by the pulp format of the magazine and the weird content of their work, these writers forged with one another and, to a lesser extent, with their readers an alternative class whose hierarchy was based not on wealth and social power, but on creativity, imagination, and the ability to craft unique stories. It is, perhaps, a testament to these writers that they were wrong in one way: their work continues to make inroads into the literary canon and is finally receiving long-overdue critical attention.

## Bibliography


Bloch, Robert. "About Our Authors," *Weird Tales*, September 1934.

Buhle, Paul. "Dystopia as Utopia: Howard Phillips Lovecraft and the Unknown Content of American Horror Literature," in *H. P. Lovecraft: Four Decades of Criticism*, ed. S. T. Joshi (Athens: Ohio University Press, 1980).

Carney, Jason. "The Shadow Modernism of Weird Tales: Experimental Pulp Fiction in the Age of Modernist Reflection" (PhD diss., Case Western Reserve University, 2014).

Csicsery-Ronay Jr., Istvan. *The Seven Beauties of Science Fiction* (Middletown, CT: Wesleyan University Press, 2008).

Earle, David M. *Re-covering Modernism: Pulps, Paperbacks, and the Prejudice of Form.* (Farnham, UK: Ashgate, 1998).

Farnese, Harold S. "The Greatest Genius," *Weird Tales*, July 1937.

Hall, Clifton. "Happy vs. Unhappy Endings," *Weird Tales*, December 1937.

Hemken, Gertrude. "Here It Is," *Weird Tales*, December 1937.

Hemken, Gertrude. "Trudy Answers Our Critics," *Weird Tales*, August–September 1936.

Howard, Robert E. *Kull: Exile of Atlantis*, ed. Patrice Louinet (New York: Ballantine, 2006).

Howard, Robert E. "Queen of the Black Coast," in *The Coming of Conan the Cimmerian*, ed. Patrice Louinet (New York: Ballantine, 2003).

Joshi, S. T. and David E. Schultz, *An H. P. Lovecraft Encyclopedia* (Westport, CT: Greenwood Press, 2001).

Kneale, James. "From Beyond: H. P. Lovecraft and the Place of Horror," *Cultural Geographies* 13, no. 1 (2006).

Nielson, Leon. *Robert E. Howard: A Collector's Descriptive Bibliography of American and British Hardcover, Paperback, Magazine, Special and Amateur Editions, with a Biography* (London: McFarland, 2007).

Finn, Mark. *Blood and Thunder: The Life and Art of Robert E. Howard* (Austin, TX: Monkeybrain, 2006).

Lemer, Marshal. "Is This Sarcasm?," *Weird Tales*, August–September 1936.

Lovecraft, H. P. "The Horror at Red Hook," in *The Dreams in the Witch House and Other Weird Stories*, ed. S. T. Joshi (New York: Penguin Classics, 2004).

Lovecraft, H. P. *Lord of a Visible World: An Autobiography in Letters*, ed. S. T. Joshi and David E. Schultz (Athens: Ohio University Press, 2000).

Lovecraft, H. P. *Selected Letters 1929–1931*, ed. August Derleth and Donald Wandrei (Sauk City, WI: Arkham House, 1971).

Lovecraft, H. P. "Supernatural Horror in Literature," in *At the Mountains of Madness: The Definitive Edition* (New York: Modern Library, 2005), 105.

Lovecraft, H. P. "The Unnamable," in *The Dreams in the Witch House and Other Weird Stories,* ed. S. T. Joshi (New York: Penguin Classics, 2004).

Lovecraft, H. P. and Robert E. Howard. *A Means to Freedom: The Letters of H. P. Lovecraft and Robert E. Howard,* ed. S. T. Joshi, David E. Schultz, and Rusty Burke (New York: Hippocampus Press, 2009).

Poe, Edgar Allan. *Poetry, Tales, and Selected Essays* (New York: Library of America, 1996).

B. M. Reynolds. "A New High Mark," *Weird Tales*, September 1934.

Shklovsky, Viktor. "Art as Technique," in *Literary Theory: An Anthology*, ed. Julie Rivkin and Michael Ryan, 2nd ed. (Maiden, MA: Blackwell Publishing, 2004).

Weinberg, Robert. *The "Weird Tales" Story* (Rockville, MD: Borgo Press, 1999).

Wilson, G. M. "Does Virtue Always Win?," *Weird Tales*, October 1937.

Wright, Farnsworth. Untitled introduction to "The Eyrie," *Weird Tales*, October 1937.

# UNKNOWABLE KNOWLEDGE: THE COMBINATION OF MATHEMATICS AND THE SUPERNATURAL IN LOVECRAFT'S "THE DREAMS IN THE WITCH HOUSE"

Howard Phillips Lovecraft is best known for his short stories and novellas about terrifying supernatural creatures of ancient and unspeakable power. Compared with stories of monsters such as Great Cthulhu and the terrible Deep Ones, far subtler stories such as Lovecraft's "The Dreams in the Witch House" seem almost insignificant. After he wrote the story, Lovecraft shared it with his pupil and friend, August Derleth, whose reaction to the story led Lovecraft to protest, "your reaction to 'Dreams in the Witch House' is, in kind, about what I expected—although I hardly think it *quite* as bad as you found it."[233] Judging by the comments he must have made, Derleth did not understand the subtlety of the story, which makes use of the space between superstition and mathematics to create a terrifyingly uncanny story. Although magic and mathematics appear to be opposites, Lovecraft's story blends the two, using them to explore what both repress: that there is knowledge and power beyond what both can contain.

"The Dreams in the Witch House" introduces the central tension of the plot in the first sentence: "Whether the dreams brought on the fever or the fever brought on the dreams Walter Gilman did not know."[234] The true nature of the terrifying dreams the protagonist, Walter Gilman, experiences remains ambiguous until the story's end: Gilman's dreams and his increasing agitation appear to be the result of his ill-advised studies in folklore and theoretical mathematics. As the story progresses, the narrative blurs the line between reality and fantasy. The plot itself, as it refuses to explain whether Gilman's dreams are real, reflects this central tension. In the story mathematics and superstition, which at first seem to be mutually exclusive, mix to lead the story itself. They led Gilman through his studies, to a terrifying conclusion.

Walter Gilman, a student, is fascinated by stories of the occult, and he specifically seeks out a house that was the residence of the witch Keziah Mason.[235] Gilman clearly takes pleasure from the uncanny: "Gilman believed

---

[233] Quoted in H. P. Lovecraft *The Dreams in the Witch House and Other Weird Stories.* Ed. S. T. Joshi. New York: Penguin Books, 2004, 443.

[234] Ibid., 300.

[235] Ibid., 300.

strange things about Keziah, and had felt a queer thrill on learning that her dwelling was still standing."[236] Upon renting an apartment in the house, Gilman searches the house and the places Keziah Mason was known to frequent for something to support his love for the uncanny: "He studied the timber and plaster walls for traces of cryptic designs at every accessible spot where the paper had peeled… He also rowed out twice to the ill-regarded island in the river."[237] Despite his careful search, it is not until he contracts brain-fever that the dreams and the terrors begin.[238] This suggests that the dreams are fever-induced, rather than brought on by supernatural forces, but this safe explanation becomes increasingly untenable as the story progresses.

It is important to note that, even before his illness, Gilman visits the places that later become so horrible to him: the attic apartment, the narrow, ancient lanes of Arkham, and the cursed island in the river. Nothing befalls him on these first visits; it is not until he studies the former dwelling of the witch Keziah Mason with the mathematics that he learns at his university that he contracts the fever and begins to experience the maddening dream-travels which lead to his destruction. His predisposition toward seeking out the uncanny, as evidenced by his explorations, makes him particularly vulnerable to the suggestive power of his dreams, or else to the unearthly forces which threaten him.

In his letters, Lovecraft makes it clear that he believes that witchcraft is literally practiced. For him, the "witch-cult" is an actual existing tradition with its own ceremonies and tenets. In this, he relies strongly on Margaret Murray's 1921 book *The Witch-Cult in Western Europe*. In a letter to Robert E. Howard, Lovecraft writes,

> *Something actual was going on under the surface*, so that people really stumbled on *concrete experiences* from time to time which confirmed all they had ever heard of the witch species. In brief, scholars now recognize that all through history a secret cult of degenerate nature-worshipers, furtively recruited from the peasantry and sometimes from decadent characters of more select origin, has existed throughout northwestern Europe.[239]

He stresses that the offer of knowledge and power drew many to the "witch-cults," "recruiting many degenerate and discontented people since it promised them so many more simple, understandable, and available boons than did Christianity. It was always waiting, ready to catch anybody who grew

---

[236] Ibid., 301.

[237] Ibid., 302.

[238] Ibid., 303.

[239] H. P. Lovecraft and Robert E. Howard, A Means to Freedom: The Letters of H. P. Lovecraft and Robert E. Howard, ed. S. T. Joshi, David E. Schultz, and Rusty Burke (New York: Hippocampus Press, 2009), 69. Emphasis in original.

tired of the ethics and aesthetics of the ruling European civilization."[240] Gilman, it seems, falls partially into this model, though he is driven more by curiosity than antisocial beliefs. Far from being satisfied with the "simple, understandable" truths the supernatural offers, Gilman seeks to know even more through science.

In addition to his interest in the supernatural, Gilman is a keen student of mathematics. His combined studies are clearly linked to his mental disorder and demise in the text: "Possibly Gilman ought not to have studied so hard. Non-Euclidean calculus and quantum physics are enough to stretch any brain; and when one mixes them with folklore, ... one can hardly expect to be wholly free of mental tension."[241] The story suggests that Keziah Mason made the same connection between magic and mathematics: "Old Keziah, [Gilman] reflected, might have had excellent reasons for living in a room with peculiar angles; for was it not through certain angles that she claimed to have gone outside the boundaries of the world of space we know?"[242]

After contracting the brain fever, Gilman dreams of "plunges through limitless abysses of inexplicably coloured light and bafflingly disordered sound"[243]. Beyond these abysses, he comes to two separate unearthly dimensions: the first is a green-hued world in which he cannot even stand,[244] and the second is a hideous city of grotesque creatures from whence he carries a carving into the normal world.[245] Gilman seems to travel through that abyss, which he identifies as the fourth dimension linking every possible dimension together, twice to the garrote above his attic room[246] and once to the streets of Arkham.[247] His journey through the abyss corresponds to his own scientific explanation of travel between dimensions: "Such a step, he said, would require only two stages: first, a passage out of the three-dimensional space we know, and second, a passage back to the three-dimensional sphere at another point, perhaps one of infinite remoteness."[248] The mathematical nature of these spaces is stressed by the focus on their geometry and tremendous dimensions. His unusual studies appear to explain his journeys, although he continues to rationalize them away as merely dreams.

Folklore and the study of non-Euclidian calculus are together a recipe for the uncanny in the story, and Lovecraft chose these two elements well. Both represent the same fundamental search for unexplained and unexplainable

---

240 Ibid., 71.
241 Lovecraft, *Witch House*, 300-301.
242 Ibid., 303.
243 Ibid., 304.
244 Ibid., 311.
245 Ibid., 314.
246 Ibid., 317 and 327.
247 Ibid., 323.
248 Ibid., 307.

truth beyond: folklore is the closest study of the supernatural that a University student can attempt within his curriculum, and the unusual branch of non-Euclidean calculus concerns itself with the mathematical laws of theoretical worlds that break the most fundamental geometric laws of the rational world. Both can, of course, be studied independently without ill effects, but the combination of the two, Lovecraft suggests, is a diabolical formula, since they both deal with the possibility that what we know of the world is only a glimpse of a vast, absolute reality.

Freud's theory about the uncanny explains that "It may be that the uncanny is something familiar that has been repressed and then reappears,"[249] demonstrating how the combination of these fields of knowledge create an uncanny effect. They are each repressed in each other: superstition represses the rational mind by insisting on magical processes which break fundamental scientific laws, and mathematics theorizes that everything can be explained with rational terms, and therefore dismisses the evidence of the supernatural. Both studies also share another mode of repression. Their repression extends to the repression of the very notion that, as Hamlet says it, "there are more things in heaven and earth... than are dreamt of in your philosophy," which is to say that there are truths that the human mind simply cannot and should not understand through any means.

Since neither mathematics nor superstition alone are enough to transport Gilman into the fourth dimension, the two must be combined to produce the uncanny effect. The angles in his attic room by themselves, although strange, give him no glimpse of the witch or her hideous familiar Brown Jenkin: "No ghostly Keziah flitted through the sombre halls and chambers, no small furry thing crept into his dismal eyrie to nuzzle him."[250] It is only when he begins to study Keziah's testimony and the stories of Brown Jenkin more closely, along with the "strange, almost hypnotic effect"[251] that his study of the room's angles has on him, that the abomination makes its way into his dreams.[252]

At first, it may seem that knowledge of theoretical calculus is not necessary for the uncanny effect, as the witch and her familiar are able to travel between worlds without knowledge of mathematics. Brown Jenkin and Keziah Mason, however, are not the true matter of Gilman's dreams; they are merely the messengers that lead him to the ultimate terror, Azathoth, and are themselves usually "reserved for certain lighter, sharper dreams... just before he dropped into the fullest depths of sleep."[253] Because the familiar

---

[249] Sigmund Freud, *The Uncanny*, trans. David McLintock (New York: Penguin Books, 2003): 152.
[250] Lovecraft, *Witch House*, 302.
[251] Ibid., 303.
[252] Ibid., 304.
[253] Ibid., 305.

and the witch are grounded in superstition, rather than being part of both ancient magical knowledge and modern scientific understanding, they are only a piece of the horror. To them, the travel is not uncanny, and they appear to travel between dimensions at will, suffering none of the horror or denial that Gilman does. The science of extra-dimensional travel, along with what he learns from the magic of Keziah, is what proves to be his uncanny undoing.

The unearthly knowledge Gilman uncovers is not wholly madness. If it was, it would not be uncanny, since it would have a psychological explanation. Far from destroying his faculties, his knowledge sharpens them. Walter Gilman solves the problem of theoretical physics that separates dimensions, much to the amazement of his peers.[254] During a "discussion of possibly freakish curvatures in space, and of theoretical points of approach or even contact between our part of the cosmos and various other regions,"[255] Gilman demonstrates to the university that "a man might—given mathematical knowledge admittedly beyond all likelihood of human acquirement—step deliberately from the earth to any other celestial body."[256] This moment of mathematical explanation, although it has little to do with the plot, underlines the fundamental base of the story. Gilman's knowledge of the supernatural helps him solve a mathematical formula. By combining the two forms of knowledge, Gilman sees that which was never meant for human minds: that there is more to the world than normal thought allows.

This essay has treated superstition and scientific mathematics as two viable forms of knowledge, but it is important to consider that the narrator of "The Dreams in the Witch House" gives little credence to tradition and superstition, while championing rational thought. The narrator describes the superstitious immigrants who live in Gilman's neighborhood as "simple,"[257] even "clod-like."[258] If the argument that the combination of superstition and mathematics creates the uncanny in the story is true, then superstition, too, must be an accurate source of knowledge, rather than being composed of "theories too wild and fantastic for sober credence,"[259] as the narrator says. Despite the narrator's fear and disdain, tradition is a source of strength in the story.

Perhaps the best evidence for the power can be found in superstition is in the role of the silver crucifix. It is given by the landlord, Joe Mazurewicz, to Gilman, who wears it during his final confrontation with the hideous old woman who can only be Keziah Mason. Gilman, who clings to rational belief

---

[254] Ibid., 306-307.
[255] Ibid., 307.
[256] Ibid., 307.
[257] Ibid., 320.
[258] Ibid., 325.
[259] Ibid., 334.

despite his dreams, doubts the crucifix's power when Joe offers it to him, and Joe can only force one on him "with difficulty."[260] Gilman wonders whether the cross will be of any use even as he wrestles with the witch: "He felt the chain of the crucifix grinding into his neck, and in his peril wondered how the sight of the object would affect the evil creature."[261] Gilman does make use of the crucifix, and it proves effective, panicking the witch enough for Gilman to get loose and kill her with the chain of the crucifix itself.[262] Although he does not know at the time that she is dead, the fading of the violet light reveals it to be the case,[263] and it is another—presumably Catholic—tenant's prayers against the evil that seem to return Gilman to the real world.[264] Since the crucifix and the prayers of superstitious foreigners are what save Gilman, at least temporarily, the traditional knowledge they represent is not as useless as the narrator implies.

Timothy Evans agrees that tradition is a legitimate source of knowledge and power in Lovecraft's writing in the article "A Last Defense against the Dark: Folklore, Horror, and the Uses of Tradition in the Works of H. P. Lovecraft." He writes that, "For Lovecraft, the preservation and invention of tradition were the answer to the crisis of modernity."[265] Lovecraft, who was "a devoted student and defender of his New England heritage," was "[m]otivated by an antimodernist rejection of industrial capitalism and everything that surrounded it."[266] It can be deduced that for Lovecraft, who sought out the traditional legacy of New England, the presence of witchcraft was a dilemma: far from the evils of the modern world, he considered witchcraft an evil of an ancient one. It is worth stressing that Lovecraft's witches recreate the familiar misogynistic position demonizing women with an oral tradition that is at odds with patriarchal forms of knowledge and power. Lovecraft finds the answer in tradition also, in the protection against witchcraft and the supernatural that tradition offers.

When both are combined, however, they break down the order created by both worlds through their mutual incompatibility. Together, they are chaos. This is why Azathoth, the ultimate evil, is described in the story as "the mindless entity Azathoth, which rules all time and space from a curiously environed black throne at the center of Chaos."[267] Azathoth is both mindless,

---

[260] Ibid., 321.

[261] Ibid., 328.

[262] Ibid., 328.

[263] Ibid., 329.

[264] Ibid., 329-330.

[265] Timothy H. Evans, "A Last Defense Against the Dark: Folklore, Horror, and the Uses of Tradition in the Works of H. P. Lovecraft," *Journal of Folklore Research* 42, no. 1: 128, accessed February 15, 2017, http://search.ebscohost.com/login.aspx?direct=true&db=edsgbc&AN=edsgcl.132297607.

[266] Ibid., 100.

[267] Lovecraft, *Witch House,* 319.

thereby undermining the value all of rationality and thought, and a being of Chaos, destroying all systems of order. Azathoth's chaotic influence is clearly felt in Gilman's suffering on his last night alive, when none of the others "knew what to make of the whole chaotic business."[268] In the story, the ultimate truth of the cosmos is insanity, and order is only an illusion created by knowing only part of that truth. When too much knowledge strips away that illusion, only madness, terror, and destruction result.

Gilman's problem, then, is not that he knows too little about the workings of the universe, but that he knows too much. Neither superstition nor mathematics can completely explain the fundamental laws of the world, but by attempting to make sense of those laws by using both, Gilman breaks down the order that both project over the universe and leads himself to his own demise. The danger of an excess of knowledge is underlined by how Gilman attempts to dispel the fear his unnatural dreams bring him. He "browsed aimlessly through the lighter magazines" of the public library and "killed the time at a cheap cinema show."[269] To clear his mind of the troubling truths that he has unleashed, he seeks to deaden his mind with cheap amusements that demand no advanced understanding or deeper examination. These knowledge-deadening things are his only remedy for his suffering, an attempt to alleviate the threat of the uncanny by returning to a world where nothing is ambiguous or subversive to the order of his knowledge of the world.

Returning to Freud's theories, it is now worth exploring again what is repressed and returns in "The Dreams in the Witch House." The existence of knowledge that the human mind cannot comprehend is one such uncanny return. Freud also claims that the "haunted house" is inherently uncanny and is linked to the repressed fear of death.[270] This theory has strong evidence in the story, where the house is reputedly haunted by the ghost of the witch. The story goes a step farther, however, as it implies that the witch may be very much alive, having survived outside of time and space. As Gilman explains through his studies, "One might, for example, pass into a timeless dimension and emerge at some remote period of earth's history as young as before."[271] Therefore, Keziah Mason represents the fear of death, and that fear returns as she reappears, at least in the dreams of Walter Gilman. Whether the witch herself has survived remains unclear, until the end of the story.

To understand the core issues of the text, it is important to note the inspirations for "The Dreams in the Witch House." The works of Edgar Allan Poe had an unparalleled influence on Lovecraft; Lovecraft himself

---

[268] Ibid., 330.
[269] Ibid., 316.
[270] Freud, *Uncanny*, 148.
[271] Lovecraft, *Witch House*, 322.

writes in a letter to horror writer J. Vernon Shea, "Poe has probably influenced me more than any other one person."[272] The parallels between Poe and Lovecraft are clear in this story: the protagonist suffers from an "exaggerated sense of hearing,"[273] just as the narrators of "The Tell-Tale Heart" and "The Fall of the House of Usher" do. The other connection is with Charlotte Perkins Gilman, specifically her inescapable short story, "The Yellow Wallpaper." Lovecraft "prais[ed] her for 'ris[ing] to a classic level' in her delineation of madness."[274] The connection between protagonists who go mad because of odd angles in walls or wallpaper, respectively, is made all the more evident by the name of Lovecraft's protagonist.

The connections to "The Fall of the House of Usher" and "The Yellow Wallpaper" shed light on the literal uncanny space produced by the combination of superstition and mathematics in Lovecraft. In the story, Gilman's travels through space and time are facilitated through unnatural angles; specifically, the angles formed by where "the down-slanting ceiling met the inward-slanting wall."[275] The idea that an angle could be evil and unnatural seems ludicrous to the modern reader; geometry is among the least threatening studies imaginable. Upon consideration, geometry fits perfectly into the uncanny effect that Lovecraft creates. The angles of this dimension, the way gravity, for and structure work, are an inherent and unquestioned part of the world. The instinctive knowledge of their workings is so natural that no normal human ever considers it. It is all the more unsettling, therefore, to consider a dimension in which forms that simply should not be are, where the very angles are unspeakably wrong. Kneale describes what he calls Lovecraft's "theme of 'cosmic terror'; the vast gulfs of space and time revealed by sciences like astronomy and geology [which have] no human scale."[276] "Neither magic nor science can make these things human and familiar."[277] The knowledge that Gilman glimpses through his study of "magic" and "science" is impossible for a human to understand. This is, in the most basic sense of this argument, the uncanny: to function in any sane way, a human must forget that there are things that cannot be understood by the human mind, and the discovery of these repressed truths is terrifyingly destructive and uncanny.

---

[272] H.P. Lovecraft, quoted in S. T. Joshi *A Dreamer and a Visionary: H. P. Lovecraft in His Time* (Liverpool: Liverpool UP, 2001): 141.

[273] Lovecraft, *Witch House*, 303.

[274] Golden, quoted in Julie Bates Dock, et al., "'But One Expects That': Charlotte Perkins Gilman's 'The Yellow Wallpaper' and the Shifting Light of Scholarship," *PMLA* 111, no. 1 (1996): 59, accessed February 15, 2017, www.jstor.org/stable/463133.

[275] Lovecraft, *Witch House*, 303.

[276] James Kneale, "From Beyond: H. P. Lovecraft and the Place of Horror." *Cultural Geographies* 13, no. 1 (2006): 109, http://search.ebscohost.com/login.aspx?direct=true&db=asn&AN=19149638.

[277] Ibid., 110.

The form of the story mirrors the themes and events of the story itself. The story begins by explaining away the uncanny events, and it does so convincingly: it seems overwhelmingly likely that Gilman's dreams are indeed just hallucinations brought on by his fever and fed by his interests in calculus and the supernatural. The story's explanations, reflecting Gilman's own reasoning, become increasingly unconvincing, however, as the narrator provides increasing counter-arguments. He explains his disappearances at night with sleep-walking, even though he was "barefoot and with only his night-clothes on."[278] Later, he explains the presence of the bizarre carving from his dream in his bedroom by claiming that he must have seen it somewhere in the city, although "he did not recall seeing it in any museum in Arkham."[279] The narrator can find no explanation at all for Gilman's first dream-journey to the chamber above his room: "Where Gilman could have been, how he got back to his room without making tracks in the hall, and how the muddy, furniture-like prints came to be mixed with his in the garret chamber, were wholly beyond conjecture."[280] The same lack of explanation repeats for Gilman's final journey, and the last pages of the story take the progression still further: with all rational explanations exhausted, the most irrational explanation not only surfaces, but is confirmed by the hideous bones found in the wreckage of the witch-house.

The effect and composition of the story is complex, but the basis of it is fairly straightforward. There are things in the world that yet escape the knowledge of humans, and ignorance of them is a protection that, when removed by an excess of knowledge, destroys the poor individual unlucky enough to stumble upon it.

Had "The Dreams in the Witch House" ended with the death of Gilman, even with the heart bored out of him, even with the terrible, unexplainable fragment that he woke to find in his bed, it might have been merely enjoyably uncanny, as the truth of the matter would never have been fully known. But the true horror of the world, Lovecraft reveals through the story's shocking revelation, is not in the unknown, but in the known. Like Gilman, whose forbidden knowledge leads to terrifying journeys, blasphemous ceremonies, and a hideous death, the reader is forced to acknowledge a truth more unsettling than the mere imagination could conjure: the terrors of the real world are far more threatening than those of the restless and fanciful mind. It would seem foolish to suggest that Azathoth and Yog-Sothoth lurk between the stars, but there are certainly things unexplained and maddening in this world that need no fiction to encourage them.

Whether or not the reader accepts that these supernatural horrors are real, the fear was real enough for Lovecraft. Both of his parents suffered from

---

[278] Lovecraft, *Witch House*, 308.
[279] Ibid., 317.
[280] Ibid., 324.

mental illnesses: his father "was declared legally insane when Howard was three"[281] and his mother was "mentally disturbed."[282] Lovecraft's fear that he would succumb to the same was constant. Nelson writes, "The recurring images in his works suggest rather that engulfment by the unconscious remained a continually threatening possibility to his restless consciousness."[283] He claimed the nightmare creatures he wrote about tormented his dreams; as he wrote to a friend, "I began to have nightmares of the most hideous description, peopled with things which I called 'night-gaunts'…. In dreams they were wont to whirl me through space at a sickening rate of speed, the while fretting & impelling me…."[284] Lovecraft himself was an atheist who believed that the vast cosmos held secrets unknowable to man, who was completely irrelevant in the grand scheme. In his writings, he brought forth the horror of being a mote at the mercy of unimaginable powers.

One of the central tensions in "The Dreams in the Witch House" is the destabilization of the psyche created by knowledge comprised of both mathematical and supernatural understanding. By studying science with its rational explanation for everything and folklore with its emphasis on the unknowable, Gilman creates an uncanny effect. He connects together knowledge that is both external and internal, linking two conflicting means of knowing that function as each other's repressed knowledges. Thus, he creates a recursive loop of the uncanny that, rather than cancelling itself out, points him towards a combined totality of knowledge that reveals secrets not meant for human understanding. As such, the things Gilman learns visibly strain the dominant ideologies in all forms: he, as an educated white man, is the most vulnerable to this dissolution. Western patriarchal hierarchies of time, progress, sex, and rationality are all broken down.

## Bibliography

Dock, Julie Bates, et al. "'But One Expects That': Charlotte Perkins Gilman's 'The Yellow Wallpaper' and the Shifting Light of Scholarship." *PMLA* 111, no. 1 (1996): 52-65. Accessed February 15, 2017. www.jstor.org/stable/463133

Evans, Timothy H. "A Last Defense Against the Dark: Folklore, Horror, and the Uses of Tradition in the Works of H. P. Lovecraft." *Journal of*

---

[281] Victoria Nelson, "H.P. Lovecraft and the Great Heresies," *Raritan* 15, no. 3 (1996): 93, accessed February 15 2017, http://search.ebscohost.com/login.aspx?direct=true&db=a9h&AN=9602273016.
[282] Ibid., 93.
[283] Ibid., 108.
[284] Quoted in Nelson, 98.

*Folklore Research* 42, no. 1 (2005): 99-135. Accessed February 15, 2017. http://search.ebscohost.com/login.aspx?direct=true&db=edsgbc&AN =edsgcl.132297607

Freud, Sigmund. *The Uncanny.* Translated by David McLintock. New York: Penguin Books, 2003.

Kneale, James. "From Beyond: H. P. Lovecraft and the Place of Horror." *Cultural Geographies* 13, no. 1 (2006): 106-126. Accessed February 15, 2017. http://search.ebscohost.com/login.aspx?direct=true&db=asn&AN=19 149638

Lovecraft, H.P. *The Dreams in the Witch House and Other Weird Stories.* Ed. S. T. Joshi. New York: Penguin Books, 2004.

Lovecraft, H.P. and Robert E. Howard. *A Means to Freedom: The Letters of H. P. Lovecraft and Robert E. Howard,* ed. S. T. Joshi, David E. Schultz, and Rusty Burke (New York: Hippocampus Press, 2009).

Nelson, Victoria. "H.P. Lovecraft and the Great Heresies." *Raritan* 15, no. 3 (1996): 92-122. *Academic Search Premier.* Accessed February 15, 2017. http://search.ebscohost.com/login.aspx?direct=true&db=a9h&AN=96 02273016

# THE HORROR OF ABJECTION IN "THE COLOUR OUT OF SPACE"

Semiotics shows that the signifying system through which we understand the world is based in difference—to use Derrida's term, this is based on differance. This process makes it possible for us to create concepts themselves. As Derrida writes, "Every concept is necessarily and essentially inscribed in a chain or system, within which it refers to another and to other concepts, by the sytematic play of differences. Such a play, then—differance—is no longer simply a concept, but the possibility of conceptuality, of the conceptual system and process in general."[285] Thus, essential divisions between animate and inanimate, between human and animal and plant, between understanding and ignorance form some of the strongest and most important bases of the ideology that shapes the world as we understand it, which also shapes our sense of ourselves and the very idea that we exist. All of this, even the existence of the self, therefore rests upon the necessity of there being differences that we can understand in a world that we can know. H. P. Lovecraft's "The Colour Out of Space" is based upon the threat that even this most basic of truths could be shaken. In the events of the story, a material that defies all human categories comes to Earth and devastates a farmstead by changing all things it touches to brittle, grey matter. As David Simmons touches on in regards to other Lovecraft storiess, this abject effect breaks down the sense of self; in "The Coulour Out of Space," it literally deconstructs the body of the self itself, as bodies of those afflicted by this designifying entity from beyond out world literally disintegrate.

In a recent article, David Simmons (2013) argues that the effect created by the horrors encountered by the characters in H. P. Lovecraft's horror stories should not be read as sublime, as they have been, but according to Julia Kristeva's concept of the abject. Simmons explains that the sublime, both for Burke and Kant, leads to an elevation of the one experiencing it, a reaffirmation of the ineffable imagination of the human being, while in Lovecraft the unspeakable disruption created by contact with cosmic horror has the opposite effect: it profoundly destabilizes the imagined place of humanity in the cosmos.[286] The abject violates the boundaries that secure the

[285] Jacques Derrida, 2004, "Différance" in *Literary Theory: An Anthology*, eds. Julie Rivkin and Michael Ryan, 2nd ed. Malden: Blackwell, 286.

[286] David Simmons, 2013, "'A Certain Resemblance': Abject Hybridity in H. P. Lovecraft's Short Fiction," in *New Critical Essays on H. P. Lovecraft*, ed. David Simmons, New York: Palgrave Macmillan, 18.

perceived superiority of all that secures Lovecraft's white, male, academic protagonists as the preeminent authorities in their world. According to Kristeva, the abject simultaneously brings into being and opposes the "I", the self: "Even before things for him are—hence before they are signifiable—he drives them out, dominated by drive as he is, and constitutes his own territory, edged by the abject."[287] Being exposed to the unspeakable truths of the universe, a universe in which the human construct is meaningless and worthless, produces a powerful effect of shock, horror, and alienation that is profoundly abject. As Kristeva explains, "the jettisoned object, is radically excluded and draws me toward the place where meaning collapses."[288] Simmons particularly focuses on race in "Facts Concerning the Late Arthur Jermyn" and "Under the Pyramids," demonstrating how both stories fracture the concept of white male supremacy using abject miscegenation and the abject mother. While Simmons does not examine it in his article, it is rewarding to apply this line of thinking to "The Colour Out of Space," demonstrating how the destabilizing effect of the uncategorizable material from space produces an abject effect that spreads to every kind of matter, breaking down every semiotic division on which the ideological superiority of Lovecraft—and, by extension, privileged white male Americans—is based.

Simmons's article demonstrates how the abject functions in Lovecraft as a place of anxiety. Simmons shows that Lovecraft flattened the concept of African identity to an aesthetic Other signified by its difference from his own identity, becoming a "self-reflexive expression of Lovecraft's deep-seated anxieties concerning his own American nationality and subjectivity."[289] While recognizing the potential limitations of this approach, Simmons situates Lovecraft in the tradition of the Gothic and draws on the broad field of criticism that situates the confrontation with abjection as the key element of Gothic horror. For Lovecraft, these horrors were based in the fragility of his own identity.

Simmons explains that, rather than entering into a debate about the origin and nature of Lovecraft's racism, he seeks to understand the use of the Other in Lovecraft's work, arguing that Lovecraft's "prejudiced comments belie a deeper and considerably more multifaceted engagement with concepts of the non-Western Other, a stance that is attracted to that which it is simultaneously repulsed by."[290] Simmons demonstrates that the racial abjection in Lovecraft's stories stems from a latent avowal of the anxiety that,

---

Donald Burleson, 2016, *H. P. Lovecraft: A Critical Study*, revised and updated electronic edition, New York: Hippocampus Press:

[287] Julia Kristeva, 1982, *Powers of Horror*, New York: Columbia UP, 6.
[288] Ibid., 2.
[289] Simmons, "Certain Resemblance," 2.
[290] Ibid., 18.

after all, the distinction between white and non-white people is artificial—essentially, that it is a semiotic rather than a genetic division. Despite the horror that this causes for the characters, they are never able to completely deny this destabilizing truth:

> While his protagonists recurrently encounter non-Western peoples and their cultures, ostensibly rendered 'abject' by their inhumanity and lack of civilization, these self-same protagonists are more often than not unable to exorcise any sense of dominion over those they meet. Instead, they find their sense of identity fragmented by their at least partial realization of an essential communality between all peoples. Such a repeated patterning implies a degree of ideological tension: the admission of an essential racial and biological universality within humanity tempered by a reluctance to suggest any measure of approval concerning the issue.[291]

For example, Simmons identifies the source of horror in "Arthur Jermyn" as the protagonist's realization that he is descended from the abject near-human female figure of the "white ape."

Through Lovecraft's writings, Simmons argues, he sought to externalize and control the abject, displacing it through what Kristeva calls "verbal play."[292] Simmons writes that Lovecraft's approach contrasts with one most writers take: according to Kristeva's model, "The writer is able to externalize what he or she considers abject by creating objects of repulsion in the text that can then be dealt with in a more considered and effectual manner."[293] Lovecraft, however, does not seek to "deal with" them: he allows their abject influence to remain open and disturbing. In "Under the Pyramids," Harry Houdini seeks for an Egypt he imagines to be authentic, one which was shaped in his imagination by Western fictions and which will allow him to solidify his own self-image as a Westerner. He arrives to find an Egypt already partially Westernized, ironically in an attempt to make Egypt more accessible as an object for Western consumers. The horror of the secrets that Houdini experiences under the pyramid, however, has the destabilizing effect of the abject: "Houdini is unable to gain control of the abject events he has witnessed because he cannot confidently place them in any one established narrative."[294] In other words, his system of signification has proved to be inadequate, and there is no way to repair this gap. The abject cannot be reabsorbed into the self.

This effect is reversed and magnified in "The Colour Out of Space," in which the abject seems to physically insert itself into the physical body as well as the signifying system, with horrific results. The abject effect in "The

---

[291] Ibid., 19.

[292] Kristeva, *Powers of Horror*, 19.

[293] Simmons, "Certain Resemblance," 24.

[294] Ibid., 27.

Colour Out of Space" is created by the arrival of a substance from beyond the planet, on which cannot be categorized by any understood difference: it cannot be classed in any known category of matter and defies all established laws about matter's behavior. This material not only falls outside the system of categorization that exists but invalidates its very existence. Rather than an explicitly racial or biological challenge as in other stories, it is an elemental challenge, undermining the human conception of reality itself.

The substance baffles the attempts by scientists to understand it. This effect is clearly abject, as described by Kristeva: "The abject is perverse because it neither gives up nor assumes a prohibition, a rule, or a law; but turns them aside, misleads, corrupts; uses them, takes advantage of them, the better to deny them."[295] The color out of space seems to offer a material that can be measured by scientific instruments, but by doing so it only further breaks down the validity of these processes themselves. It turns the Western process of understanding against itself and destroys it.

When the material arrives in a meteorite of an unknown origin, scientists from the fictional Miskatonic University arrive to study it, to class it according to their understanding of the cosmos or to expand their understanding to fit this new substance. They can ultimately do neither. The scientists' attempt to run tests on it is described in great detail, demonstrating the concerted attempts the experts use to try to find some way to categorize the substance: "It had acted quite unbelievably in that well-ordered laboratory; doing nothing at all and shewing no occluded gases when heated on charcoal, being wholly negative in the borax bead, and soon proving itself absolutely non-volatile at any producible temperature, including that of the oxy-hydrogen blowpipe."[296] The mention of the "well-ordered laboratory" demonstrates the fundamental function of the abject in this scene: the "clean and proper"[297] laboratory, a tool for establishing a narrative with hard boundaries and delineations, is thwarted and trumped by the abject substance. Simmons argues that this rational narrative, which has at its core the concept that everything can be measured, quantified, and understood by human means, is key to the Western ability to resist the abject disintegrative force of chaos: "In these stories, the West lies precariously balanced between civilization and the chaos that would be born again if the Other were able to get a foothold."[298] The loss of that narrative upsets not only civilization itself but the very fabric of the reality crafted by human signification.

The approach but do not fully grasp this abject realization the material from space brings, trying to repress the knowledge that their tools—including

---

295 Kristeva, *Powers of Horror*, 16.
296 Lovecraft, H.P., 2002, *The Call of Cthulhu and Other Weird Stories*, London: Penguin Books, 174.
297 Kristeva, *Powers of Horror*, 108.
298 Simmons, "Certain Resemblance," 27.

their ideological apparatus—are insufficient. They are left grasping at unsolutions, still attempting to categorize the substance with their own tools and understanding, but this only underlines their failure: "when upon heating before the spectroscope it displayed shining bands unlike any known colours of the normal spectrum there was much breathless talk of new elements, bizarre optical properties, and other things which puzzled men of science are wont to say when faced by the unknown."[299] In this "breathless talk," there is the horrifyingly compelling force of the abject: it forces itself into the narrative and demands to be engaged with. The thoroughness of these tests further emphasizes that "...at the end of the tests the college scientists were forced to own that they could not place it. It was nothing of this earth, but a piece of the great outside; and as such dowered with outside properties and obedient to outside laws."[300] Their inability to quantify and identify this material, to incorporate it into the semiotic system, inspires in them a cosmic horror of a place where their understanding of reality fails: "in time the professors felt scarcely sure they had indeed seen with waking eyes that cryptic vestige of the fathomless gulfs outside; that lone, weird message from other universes and other realms of matter, force, and entity."[301] This is the most significant effect of the color out of space: not only is it abject, but it renders everything else abject as well, ungrounded and horrifying.

Kristeva explains that the abject, once a source of fascination and attraction, becomes repellant, and it makes others repellant, too: "Once upon blotted-out time, the abject must have been a magnetized pole of covetousness. But the ashes of oblivion now serve as a screen and reflect aversion, repugnance. The clean and proper (in the sense of incorporated and incorporable) becomes filthy, the sought-after turns into the banished, fascination into shame."[302] This filthiness and shame touches the academics at the university, but its full force descends on the place where the abject entity is most present, where it literally disintegrates all matter, from plant life to human, and renders it "grey and brittle."

The mention of it being a message is particularly telling: it is abject but not indecipherable, and as the people of the New England area that comes to be known as the "blasted heath" struggle to grasp its meaning, their world literally loses the distinction between types of matter even as the semiotic distinctions between them break down. The universe itself takes on an unnatural and unhealthy aspect in their minds due to the change this abject force creates in matter that felt familiar and known: "all agreed that plants of that kind ought never to sprout in a healthy world."[303] This information is

---

[299] Lovecraft, "Colour," 174.
[300] Ibid., 176.
[301] Ibid., 177.
[302] Kristeva, *Powers of Horror*, 8.
[303] Lovecraft, "Colour," 179.

imparted to the narrator by Ammi Pierce, a local farmer and the sole source of information about the events that took place years before. Ammi lives close enough to the blasted heath to know the inhabitants personally but not close enough to be physically affected—or so it seems. It is he who witnesses firsthand the disintegration of the Gardner family into "grey and brittle" masses that forms the apex of the plot.

The greyness that characterizes the victims of the color out of space removes from them the privilege of their race. Simmons connects Lovecraft's anxieties about the threat of abjection to deny them their whiteness; he writes that it "implies a degree of ideological tension: the admission of an essential racial and biological universality within humanity tempered by a reluctance to suggest any measure of approval concerning the issue"[304] and demonstrates how hybridity in stories such as "Facts Concerning the Late Arthur Jermyn and his Family" make ambiguous the division between white and non-white as well as between human and non-human. By turning humans grey, the substance removes from them the single most important marker of ideological racial superiority: the color of their skin.

Vivian Ralickas lays out the shape of this abject effect on language and the individual. She associates it with the crisis of modernity, when previous systems of signification were dethroned, with no visible successor. Part of this crisis is in cracks that were appearing around the identities Lovecraft clung to. As she writes:

> If no language exists to contextualize modernity in Lovecraft's fiction, then what is left to articulate but the shock of alienation? In realizing that its 'clean and proper' body is always already defiled, the Lovecraftian subject discovers that all of its safeguards—culture, tradition, race, ancestry, language—are forfeited. 'Cosmic horror' therefore unveils to the subject that it is simultaneously abject and abjected by the same universe in whose center it was erroneously placed by the efforts of humanism.[305]

And, indeed, the threat of modernity can well be felt in the story, as the threat arrives from space, an unknown zone just starting to be explored and identified by science. In combining this new perceived threat with the traditional American stereotype of the uncanny and evil backwoods, Lovecraft highlights a threat that modern progress threatens to unleash: the narrator comes to the blasted heath to survey for a new reservoir which threatens to spread the tainted water from the heath to the city of Arkham itself. The narrator, although hoping the reservoir will destroy the farmstead once and for all, reflects, "nothing could bribe me to drink the new city water

---

of Arkham."[306] As knowledge of the abject substance spreads to Arkham through the scientists, so too does its taint.

The word "brittle" is also important, used to describe everything from the plant life to the humans who are touched by the substance that moves around the farm. At first, only the plants seem affected: "And all the while the vegetation was turning grey and brittle. Even the flowers whose hues had been so strange were greying now, and the fruit was coming out grey and dwarfed and tasteless. The asters and goldenrod bloomed grey and distorted...."[307] Next, it affects the animals: "The swine began growing grey and brittle and falling to pieces before they died, and their eyes and muzzles developed singular alterations."[308] In the brittleness of matter touched by this abject force, we see revealed the fragility of the sense of self in the Freudian self, with its reliance on narcissism. As described by Kristeva, "Abjection, with a meaning broadened to take in subjective diachrony, is a precondition of narcissism. It is coexistent with it and causes it to be permanently brittle."[309] When, inevitably, the Gardner family living on the farm also becomes grey and brittle and ultimately succumbs, this abject disturbance comes to its full effect.

The abject affects language as well as it becomes impossible to verbalize what it represents. Kristeva shows that the corpse is the ultimate source of the abject, the most powerful means of attacking the "I": "In that compelling, raw, insolent thing in the morgue's full sunlight, in that thing that no longer matches and therefore no longer signifies anything, I behold the breaking down of a world that has erased its borders: fainting away."[310] The body itself, the most basic signifier of self, becomes abjected. These dead bodies of the Gardner family become so hideous to the narrator, their meaning so repulsive, that he can no longer refer to them in anything but abject terms: he calls the dying woman a "blasphemous monstrosity,"[311] a "horror,"[312] and in many cases "it."[313] The use of passive voice and the lack of objects also show how the subject of the victims has become transgressed, for example in the statement "There was a dry brittleness, and dry fragments were scaling off."[314] This disintegration is prefigured in the failure of language to represent the effect: "the poor woman screamed about things in the air which she could

---

306 Lovecraft, "Colour," 173.

307 Ibid., 182.

308 Ibid., 183.

309 Kristeva, *Powers of Horror*, 13.

310 Ibid., 4.

311 Lovecraft, "Horror," 187.

312 Ibid., 187.

313 Ibid., 188.

314 Ibid., 188.

not describe. In her raving there was not a single specific noun, but only verbs and pronouns."[315]

The thing that has become of Nabby Gardner proves to violate not only the distinction between human and animal but also that between life and death: "But the terrible thing about this horror was that it very slowly and perceptibly moved as it continued to crumble."[316] Even as it disintegrates into pieces that are not even organic, let alone human, Nabby continues to exhibit the traits of life. She—or it—continues to move perceptibly, communicating the horror of its existence to its observer. Just as Nabby is unable to even express the abject thing that infects her, she herself ultimately loses all markers of signification: she is rendered an abject and unnameable "thing" with no name, race, or sex. When the victims are ultimately described, they are undifferentiated, only given as "four monstrous sets of fragments."[317] The narrator finds it too horrible to describe them even as something that was once human, alive, even organic.

The mention of blasphemy, damnation, and what they implies about the continuity of a Christian framework is key to this scene, as well as to the story. Just as the abject material breaks down the divisions essential to satisfying scientific imagination at Miskatonic University, it also attacks the religious ideology that is the basis of the worldview of the rural farmers. In the telling, Ammi Pierce attempts to cling to the familiar narrative of good and evil, of heaven and hell, and to place the horribly inhuman human that Nabby has been transformed into in this simple framework. This proves impossible, however; Ammi's imagination finds itself incapable of categorizing it as such: "must all be a judgment of some sort; though he could not fancy what for, since he had always walked uprightly in the Lord's ways so far as he knew."[318] He can think of no reason to imagine the Gardners would be rightfully damned, though there is the suggestion in "as far as he knew" that even this part of his understanding of the world has completely come free from its moorings.

Even with this complete breakdown in Ammi, the story only suggests what effect the weight of the abject disintegration would have on the self if it came to those truly capable of understanding it. The scientists are too secure in their faith in their methods to be entirely disturbed, and the farmers are too simple-minded. As the narrator reminds us, "Anyone but a stolid farmer would have fainted or gone mad, but Ammi walked conscious through that low doorway and locked the accursed secret behind him."[319] Here, the narrator foregrounds another source of horror in the response of

---

[315] Ibid., 181.
[316] Ibid., 187.
[317] Ibid., 192.
[318] Ibid., 185.
[319] Ibid., 187.

the spectators to the abject disintegration of those around them. The sensitive response—indeed, the human response—would be to suffer an immediate breakdown in one's own signifying ability and the complete failure of sanity that this comes with. Kristeva describes this very threat of the abject: "A 'something' that I do not recognize as a thing. A weight of meaninglessness, about which there is nothing insignificant, and which crushes me. On the edge of nonexistence and hallucination, of a reality that, if I acknowledge it, annihilates me."[320] Perhaps, then, the miasmal substance that plagues the Gardner farm would not need to directly contact the individual to cause disintegration: in the breaking down of the ordering system itself, the self and the world around it would collapse back into each other, reversing the prime function of abjection to separate the I from the not-I. This effect later appears in the person of the narrator.

This effect is demonstrated by the double narrator frame of the story, as Ammi tells his tale to the unnamed narrator. As a "stolid farmer," Ammi demonstrates a monstrous lack of imagination, simply failing to fully comprehend the monumental designifying signification of what he has witnessed, though he is nevertheless shaken deeply. "With an associative sense goaded to feverish heights, he thought unaccountably of what he had seen upstairs. Good God! What eldritch dream-world was this into which he had blundered? He dared move neither backward nor forward, but stood there trembling at the black curve of the boxed-in staircase."[321] Tellingly, not only what he has seen sears itself into his mind, but the very mundane details of the staircase around him: "Every trifle of the scene burned itself into his brain. The sounds, the sense of dread expectancy, the darkness, the steepness of the narrow steps—and merciful heaven! . . . the faint but unmistakable luminosity of all the woodwork in sight; steps, sides, exposed laths, and beams alike!"[322] It is important to remember that these descriptions are given to us by the unnamed narrator, not Ammi, and represent the narrator's interpretation of the events—including the narrator's own utterances of horror. In the glow that now issues from even the house itself, the insidious infection of the abject material can be detected. It has now touched even the most familiar material, transforming what was known and secure into another source of horror and abjection not only for Ammi but for the narrator as well.

This transformation of the familiar demonstrates the ultimate effect of the material that came down from space in the story. What was known and categorized becomes not only unknown but unknowable. The body and its own world become strange and foreign. Kristeva describes this effect of the abject thus: "... one can understand that it [the abject] is experienced at the

---

[320] Kristeva, *Powers of Horror*, 2.
[321] Lovecraft, "Colour," 187.
[322] Lovecraft, 187.

peak of its strength when that subject, weary of fruitless attempts to identify with something on the outside, finds the impossible within; when it finds that the impossible constitutes its very being, that it is none other than abject."[323] This effect can be seen most keenly in the suggestion about the effect that lingers in the story. Not only is there the suggestion of uncleanness in the water, but the narrator worries about the end of Ammi Pierce, who plays the role of narrator to the narrator: "I would hate to think of him as the gray, twisted, brittle, monstrosity which persists more and more in troubling my sleep."[324] Donald Burleson writes that these "powerful closing lines" show that the story "is never really finished":[325] the threat of disintegration spreads as more and more become exposed to the effect of the unearthly element. Thus, the color's effects seem to spread to the rest of humanity, ready to destroy all differences upon which the fragile world is based, including race, sex, and humanity itself. To Lovecraft, mourning the demise of his Anglo-Saxon family's fortunes, the collapse of their importance brought with it a deeper horror: that the very existence of those things that made his family once so influential is supremely fragile.

Perhaps the only way to escape annihilation by this designifying knowledge is to escape into what the narrator chooses at the end of the short story: "Do not ask me for my opinion. I do not know—that is all."[326] Those familiar with Kristeva, however, perceive the ultimate threat of the story: that the narrator and the reader, now fascinated, will also succumb to the lure of the color out of space and thus to its disintegrative influence. As the dying Nahum Gardner says, words recalled by the narrator at the end of the story, "it beats down your mind an' then gits ye... can't git away... draws ye... it come from some place whar things ain't as they is here... one o' them professors said so...he was right...."[327] As shown in "The Colour Out of Space," there are no essential differences between humans, animals, plants, or even inert matter, and the horror of this lack of boundary is exposed by the matter from space that defies all of these categories. As Kristeva reminds us, "One thus understands why so many victims of the abject are its fascinated victims—if not its submissive and willing ones."[328] In Kristeva, the abject prevents the self from collapse by maintaining the signifying system, and Lovecraft reminds us just how brittle that system is as we fall into its destruction.

---

[323] Kristeva, *Powers of Horror* 5.

[324] Lovecraft, "Colour," 199.

[325] Donald R. Burleson, 2016, *H. P. Lovecraft: A Critical Study*. Revised and updated electronic edition, New York: Hippocampus Press, 158.

[326] Lovecraft, "Colour," 198.

[327] Ibid., 189.

[328] Kristeva, *Powers of Horror*, 9.

## Bibliography

Burleson, Donald R. 2016. *H. P. Lovecraft: A Critical Study*. Revised and updated electronic edition. New York: Hippocampus Press.

Derrida, Jacques. 2004. "Différance" in *Literary Theory: An Anthology*, eds. Julie Rivkin and Michael Ryan. 2nd ed. Malden: Blackwell.

Kristeva, Julia. 1982. *Powers of Horror*. New York: Columbia UP.

Lovecraft, H. P. 2002. "The Colour Out of Space" in *The Call of Cthulhu and Other Weird Stories*. London: Penguin Books.

Ralickas, Vivian. 2007. "'Cosmic Horror' and the Question of the Sublime in Lovecraft." *Journal of the Fantastic in the Arts* 18 (3): 364-398.

Simmons, David. 2013. "'A Certain Resemblance': Abject Hybridity in H. P. Lovecraft's Short Fiction." in *New Critical Essays on H. P. Lovecraft*, ed. David Simmons. New York: Palgrave Macmillan.

# HUNGARY AND HUNGARIANS IN THE WRITINGS OF ROBERT E. HOWARD

For a young man who lived all of his thirty years in and around Texas in an age before television or the internet, Robert E. Howard wrote about places and times completely removed from his own with vivid and confident prose. It is easy to be swept away into a multitude of exotic locales by his evocative writings. It is interesting to examine how Howard makes use of the often limited sources available to him to mine for interesting places both in time and space, filling them out with his own imagination and the influence of other writers. To examine Howard's world-building, it is interesting to look at his representations of one particular ethnic group he only knew through his reading.

In this paper, I will look at the three very different ways he uses the nation and people of Hungary in his stories. I will use these stories to illustrate the ways in which Howard not only used history and world cultures for inspiration but also adapted them to his own purposes. Howard relied as much on his own interpretations of historical events as on texts, and he used his imagination to paint in the gaps, sometimes even splashing some of that paint over the facts to get at the truths he felt inside the stories. This is not to say Howard was careless with facts. His research was often as extensive as his sources allowed, and his historical portrayals show a particular eye for detail.

This is partially due to Howard's ability to place himself into the worlds he writes about. As she recounts in her book *One Who Walked Alone*, Novalyne Price once asked Howard why he could speak with such authority about the fabulous tents of Genghis Khan. Howard replied, "Because I was there." His belief in reincarnation is an excellent illustration of his approach to historical fiction. For Howard, the stories from history books really happened, and he put himself into all of them, feeling deep emotions even in relatively dry texts because he could place himself into them.

In addition to his imagination, Howard's interest in historical minutiae is remarkable. He famously began his correspondence with H.P. Lovecraft by correcting the latter on some Gaelic in his story, and he worried that getting the facts right for his historical fiction took too long for him to turn a profit selling them. History provided an excellent basis and inspiration for his work, and it is as such that he used it through his career.

Using this as a model, I will examine three texts, moving in chronological order not in the order Howard wrote them but rather in the order they might have occurred historically. My primary interest is to examine how Howard used facts and references in his stories, and I will employ these to attempt to shed light on some of Howard's storytelling techniques in using different races and settings in his stories. I will look at "The Shadow of the Vulture," a historical adventure set in the Sixteenth Century in the wake of the battle of Mohács in Hungary; "Swords of the Hills," an El Borak story that takes place in the Middle East and features a Hungarian villain; and "The Black Stone," which unfolds in Hungary itself.

1934's "The Shadow of the Vulture" is set in Vienna in 1529. The invasion of Suleiman the Magnificent forms the crux of the story. The Turks, having subdued Hungary, now set their sights on Vienna. In the wake of the battle of Mohács in 1526, in which the Kingdom of Hungary was decisively defeated by the Turks, Hungary effectively ceased to be an independent nation on the European stage, though it would take many more years for Austria and Turkey to divide up the country. It was at the battle of Mohács that the story's protagonist, Gottfried von Kalmbach, struck the Sultan the wound that created their personal animosity. Historically, a charge of knights indeed come close to reaching the Sultan. Hungarian heavy cavalry stormed into the teeth of the Turkish guns and came within sight of the Sultan, so that he was removed to the rear of the battle. According to legend, Hungarian arrows struck the Sultan's cuirass, but he was never in danger of being struck by a sword—perhaps because the Hungarians, though they were well known for using foreign mercenaries in their wars, never had the assistance of Gottfried von Kalmbach.

The story makes use of the complex political situation in Hungary in the wake of the Battle of Mohács. Howard introduces the political situation in Hungary thus: "Suleyman's officers knew that the Grand Turk had more in mind than merely establishing his puppet Zapolya on the conquered Hungarian throne. Suleyman's ambitions embraced all Europe." This refers to the Transylvanian János Zápolya (or Szapolyai) who became king of Hungary after the death of the king Louis (Lajos) II at Mohács. After the battle, to which he arrived too late to take part, Szapolyai had the only intact army in Hungary and easily took the throne. As the vajda of Transylvania, he was the most politically and militarily powerful alternative to the Holy Roman Emperor, Ferdinand I. When it became obvious Szapolyai couldn't hold the country by himself, he first made a military alliance with the Turks and then became their vassal. According to Ottoman policies, this would have allowed him to rule the country with some autonomy, rather than placing himself under the complete control of the Habsburgs. After being defeated by Ferdinand I at the Battle of Tarcal, Szapolyai fled the country in 1528. He returned to the country in 1529 with Ottoman aid and ruled until 1540[329].

The grim political reality in Hungary was that there hadn't been a

---

[329] Miklós Molnár, *A Concise History of Hungary* (Cambridge: Cambridge UP, 2001).

Magyar—ethnically Hungarian—royal line since 1301. The country had been ruled by foreigners—Louis himself was Bohemian—for the last two centuries, often by the richest lord who could buy electors or by the lord with the strongest army. A brief period in which the hero János Hunyadi and his son Mátyás ruled in the 15th Century alone stands out, though the Hunyadi family was almost certainly of Wallach descent. Szapolyai, who was of a noble Hungarian family, could very well have been a better choice than the Holy Roman Emperor, regardless of what power he served.

The reasoning for the historical perspective "The Shadow of the Vulture" takes can be easily gleaned from the story's conflict. Howard sets up a simple choice between Ottoman rule and Emperor Ferdinand. This sets the stage for the vicious battle that plays out in the story, when with the help of Gottfried and Red Sonya the Austrians turn back the Ottomans and save Europe. Still, the choice between two foreign rulers for Hungary may well be reflected in Gottfried's own sentiments on kings and politics: "Zapolya is a dog because he stood aside at Mohacz, and let us, his comrades, be cut to pieces, but Ferdinand is a dog too. When I am penniless I sell him my sword. … May the devil bite me if I draw sword for any man while I have a penny left[330]."

Other minor details include a brief reference to the "iron crown of Hungary," in the typically Howardian style of iron and blood, "torn from the dead king Louis' head on the bloody field of Mohacz." The Holy Crown of Hungary is golden and jeweled, and it certainly was not carried by the king to a battlefield, though here we can assume Howard was being metaphorical. It is also notable that the king did not die on the field, but rather drowned crossing a creek swollen with runoff.

Also interesting is Howard's description of Red Sonya of Rogatino, the story's heroine, as wearing a "long Hungarian saber."[331] Though the saber would only be popularized in Poland later in the 16th century, Hungarians had been using such weapons for centuries. It's perhaps worth noting that the word "saber" itself is said to originate from the Hungarian "*szablya*," which is said to derive from the word "*szab*," meaning "to cut."

Howard's source for this history has been identified as Fairfax Downey's 1929 *The Grand Turk*. This book is based on the 1879 text *The Sieges of Vienna* by the Turks makes reference to the Hungarian king as "Zapolya," spelled the same as by Howard, and to a "Wolf Hagen," whom Howard writes of as "Wulf Hagen," recounting his brave raid on the Turkish artillery that sank it into the Danube. The book speaks in harsh terms of the Hungarian king, referring to his "mischief" and "defection" at Mohács. This slant on the Hungarian king appears in other Western texts of the time as well, and

---

[330] Robert E. Howard, *Sword Woman and Other Historical Adventures* (New York: Ballantine Books, 2011), 483.
[331] Ibid., 430.

Howard probably learned his opinion of Szapolyai from them.

Although Howard speaks in positive terms of the courage of the Hungarians at Mohács, this treatment of the Hungarian king as a spineless Ottoman puppet may well set the stage for the appearance of another Hungarian in Howard's unpublished El Borak adventure story "Swords of the Hills," which has also appeared with the title "The Lost Valley of Iskander." El Borak, also known as the American Francis Xavier Gordon, roams across the Middle East encountering mystery and danger at every turn. In this story, the primary antagonist is "Gustav Hunyadi, black sheep of a noble Magyar house." The term Magyar is the Hungarian term for Hungarians, and can also refer to the ethnicity in general. Perhaps Gustav's black sheep status extends to his first name: Gustav is certainly no Hungarian name. On the other hand, Hunyadi is a name instantly recognizable to any Hungarian.

The setting of this story is an anachronistically Greek village somewhere in the Middle East. Hunyadi the "renegade and international adventurer" plans to set up his own kingdom in this land by pitting the local chiefs against each other in civil war. This mirrors the historical János Hunyadi, a successful military commander who later became king of Hungary. As a landed and wealthy young noble, Hunyadi served the Holy Roman Emperor Sigismund in his wars against the Bohemian Hussites and the Turks. It is thus he earned the Emperor's favor and played a key role as a kingmaker after the death of Sigismund, later appointing himself regent of Hungary. Howard writes that his Hunyadi "plotted the destruction of nations," reflecting the real Hunyadi's own ambitions in ruling Hungary and expanding its influence in the face of the Turkish invasions. Hunyadi turned the Turks back in battle after battle, including the turning point at the bloody siege of Belgrade, for which great victory the Pope instituted the noonday bell throughout Europe. It is not a stretch to see a reflection in this famous siege—even though the historical Hunyadi was the one *being* besieged—when events unfold in the story that cause El Borak to say, "The walls of the city are rotten. If we try to defend them, with Hunyadi directing the siege, we will be trapped like rats." Though the fictional Hunyadi may be a villain, the traits he inherited from his historical counterpart may well explain why Howard writes that in Hunyadi El Borak "had met his match."

In this historical connection, we see another of Howard's techniques for crafting his stories, that of using historical references to create a certain resonance in his locales and characters. Setting the story in the Valley of Iskander recalls for Howard the legend of Alexander the Great and his conquests, a legend he inserts El Borak into when the American adventurer struggles against the hugely muscular local king named Ptolemy. This invites a host of historical connections in its own right. Just so, the name Hunyadi may have been Howardian shorthand for the military cunning, courage, and determination of Gustav's historical counterpart, not to mention his lust for power and to establish his own dynasty—János Hunyadi passed on the throne to his son Mátyás, who reigned as king. By connecting a fictional character to a historical figure, Howard takes a character who was ready-made, brings out the elements of him he likes, and inserts him into his plot. Thus, he gives El Borak a memorable villain to pit his strength against. And perhaps it also pleased Howard's sense of poetic irony that János Hunyadi's fictional namesake, instead of being a fabled enemy of the Turks, allies himself with Turks and Afghans. Historically as well as fictionally, the assault on the besieged defenders failed, though in the story Hunyadi is on the other side.

It is possible Howard used as inspiration for a Hungarian adventurer in the Middle East the real-life noble Lászlo Almási, who is said to have been the basis for the novel *The English Patient*. After flying in the First World War, Almási spent time in Egypt and North Africa, where he was part of an expedition searching for the mythical oasis Zerzura. He also established contact with a tribe of Africans who, according to legend, were descended from Hungarian soldiers in Turkish service who had been stationed in North Africa. The real-life exploits of such an adventurer, who was a contemporary of Howard's, could well have made an impact on the young Texan writer. Although I admit I have found no concrete connection that would show he even knew about him, men like Almási were not rare in this time. Hungary was among many countries driven to extreme poverty in this time, having lost more than two thirds of its land after the First World War, and many Hungarians, with military experience and no home to return to, turned to adventuring in foreign lands.

Beyond the obvious historical connection of the Hunyadi name and a possible reference to Hungarian adventurers, Howard reveals no familiarity with contemporary Hungarian peoples or customs in his stories. This becomes obvious in his short story "The Black Stone." This horror story, published in 1931 and intended as far as I can tell to be contemporary, draws its narrator into pagan-haunted backwoods where an ancient stone of Lovecraftian evil lurks.

We can immediately see a connection to Howard's "The Shadow of the Vulture," which was published three years later, in the historical background of the short story. The narrator passes the battlefield "Schomvaal where the brave Polish-Hungarian knight, Count Boris Vladinoff, made his gallant and futile stand against the victorious hosts of Suleiman the Magnificent, when the Grand Turk swept over eastern Europe in 1526."[332] I have been able to find no actual "Larson's *Turkish Wars*" or Boris Vladinoff. It is tempting to

---

[332] Robert E. Howard, *The Horror Stories of Robert E. Howard* (New York: Ballantine Books, 2008), 174.

speculate that, if Howard would have fleshed out the backstory a little more, we might even find mention here of Gottfried von Kalmbach and the Siege of Vienna.

While "Schomvaal" seems vaguely German, the name of the town "Stregoicavar" no doubt originates from Howard's reading of Bram Stoker's *Dracula*. In this connection I am indebted to Steve Tompkins for his article "Black Stone in a Red Setting," published in *The Chronicler of Cross Plains,* in which he traces many of the origins of the short story. The word "stregoica," spelled exactly as Howard spells it, appears in Dracula as "witch" in a list of words that are actually a jumble of Romanian and Hungarian. This seems to be based on the Romanian word "strigoaică." Howard translates Stregoicavar thus: "an ominous name, meaning something like Witch-Town." It's likely that, looking at his maps, Howard saw names of real towns such as Temesvár, a name he uses in the story, and assumed vár means town. In actuality, the vár in these place names indicates the presence of a castle, and usually indicates a city around a major border castle (*"vár"* is Hungarian for castle). Thus, naming the little Hungarian backwater Stregoicavar is something akin to naming it Witch Castle in a mix of bad Romanian and Hungarian. To be fair, Howard could hardly fact-check Bram Stoker, but I include this detail because the combination of Stoker's stregoica and his best guess at the meaning of var is an excellent example of Howard's system of borrowing and filling in gaps for the sake of the story.

As Tompkins points out, Howard greatly enjoyed Dracula, and the superstitious peasants of "The Black Stone" seem to have been drawn almost whole cloth from those of that novel[333]. They even refer to the narrator with the anachronistically German "Herr" the peasants call Jonathan Harker in Dracula. Howard is fairly kind to these peasants, however, and even writes that the schoolmaster is "a man of surprizing education."[334] Perhaps there is some wisdom in their superstition, as they keep well away from the black stone, and it is by failing to heed their advice that the story's narrator has his terrifying encounter with forces beyond his understanding. Beyond this, authentic details of Hungarian customs or architecture are notably absent from the story. Howard makes a broad guess at them with, "The quaint houses and the quainter dress and manners of the people were those of an earlier century"[335] and leaves the rest to our imagination. Here, Howard gives us just as much as he knows, and doesn't try to fill in the gaps.

Tompkins also discusses why Hungary makes such a fertile ground for such a story. It forms the Eastern boundary of the West and the Western boundary of the East, at times variously under European and Asian control,

---

[333] Steve Tompkins, "Black Stone in a Red Setting," *The Chronicler of Cross Plains* 1, no. 2 (2006). http://www.robert-e-howard.org/VGNNss03.html

[334] Howard, *Horror Stories*, 180.

[335] Ibid., 180.

and belonging at least in part to the border region of the Balkans. Thus, Hungary proves a familiar kind of Howardian shorthand for the intersection of rationality and superstition that forms the crux of the story itself.

As to the likelihood of a pagan cult in Hungary surviving until 1526 to be destroyed by the Turkish soldier-scholar Selim Bahadur, it is as likely as any Lovecraft Circle atavistic cult. Hungary was converted fairly late to Christianity, in the year 1000, and in 1048 there were still enough pagan peasants to force the current king off the throne. It is hardly a stretch to believe pagans would have survived for another 500 years in such a remote village.

As an aside, it is an entirely different matter to speculate on whether Hungarian peasants would have strayed from their historical shamanism to worship a toadlike abomination, as they do in the story, or whether such worship would have involved the mad dancing of naked girls being lashed by priests. This, I believe, calls for no historical examination.

As we have seen, Howard did more than just take a few elements that fired his fancy out of history books and fill in the rest from his inventive mind. He utilized what sources he had available to him and attempted to represent history as truly as he could manage, though he was not above coloring in some of his own facts to suit the story he was trying to tell. Borrowing historical touchpoints to build his worlds also allowed him to create the sweeping themes and conflicts he is known for. In "The Shadow of the Vulture," we see him using his own slant of Hungarian history to set up the stand of Imperial Vienna against the Turks. By using the name of the warrior and regent János Hunyadi in "The Swords of the Hills," Howard borrowed a historical figure and used some of his characteristics to help craft a convincing adversary for El Borak. And in "The Black Stone," Howard borrows from *Dracula* and, as does that novel, utilizes Hungary's position on the border of the West and the East to present the setting of a story that exists in an uncanny middle ground between rationality and superstition. In all of these stories, Howard fuses imagination and fact, using history as inspiration and the basis of the stories he built from there.

## Bibliography

Howard, Robert E. *El Borak and Other Desert Adventures*. New York: Ballantine Books, 2010.

Howard, Robert E. *The Horror Stories of Robert E. Howard*. New York: Ballantine Books, 2008.

Howard, Robert E. *Sword Woman and Other Historical Adventures*. New York: Ballantine Books, 2011.

Molnár, Miklós. *A Concise History of Hungary*. Cambridge: Cambridge UP, 2001.

Steve Tompkins, "Black Stone in a Red Setting," The Chronicler of Cross Plains 1, no. 2 (2006). http://www.robert-e-howard.org/VGNNss03.html

# "I WAS A MAN BEFORE I WAS A KING": AN EXAMINATION OF CONAN'S KINGSHIP THROUGH THE POLITICAL THEORY OF GIORGIO AGAMBEN

Though he is popularly known as a barbarian, Conan is introduced to the reader in his first story as a king. Far from being simply an end point to Conan's career, his kingship is an inherent part of who he is. The theories of political theorist Giorgio Agamben shed light on why and how a warrior and an outlaw might rise to such a position by exploring the roles of the king and bandit in society. According to Agamben, both the king and the bandit exist partially outside the two sides that constitute a state: the king is part of the state but not subject to it, while the bandit is outside the state but subject to it. As such, the two share a powerful link. Conan from king to bandit and back again, but never lives both within a state and subject to its laws, as a figure like Conan can never simply be the subject of a state. As such, Conan can be imagined not only as a perpetual outsider but also as a man who draws power from always occupying a marginal role. Thus, the Conan stories question the theory of social contract on which the United States of America was founded and reveal an interesting anxiety related to democracy and power, an anxiety that can be clearly connected to the Great Depression, including the tremendous wealth disparity it revealed and the social unrest it caused.

The theories put forward in Agamben's *Homo sacer* illustrate that the sovereign's power comes from his the ability to suspend the law, killing at will. This idea challenges the notion that sovereignty comes from the consent of the governed; Agamben argues that it comes from the ability to exercise violence in a specific way. While the law has provisions for executing criminals, the sovereign can completely suspend the law and kill those he deems bandits at will. The way Conan's kingship is portrayed matches Agamben's theories well, creating surprising connections between Robert E. Howard's writing and modern political theory. Conan is a bandit who takes and keeps the throne of Aquilonia. He is simultaneously one who deals violence and is at risk of violence. As such, Conan embodies Agamben's concept of the zone of indistinction between sovereign and *homo sacer*, the man who can be killed by anyone.

Conan embodies this concept best as king; however, there are some who consider Conan's kingship uninteresting. In his essay "King Kull as a Prototype for Conan," Darrell Schweitzer writes that "One doubts that

Conan's or Kull's reigns would be very successful either..." and "the hero's 'good old days' made a better story than his kingship, which could only consist of ... the barbarian king fending off one rebellion or assassination after another."[336] Schweitzer argues that the "*real story*" of these characters is that of the life of the adventurer[337], and was a "mistake" for Howard to write about Conan or Kull as a king, since these tie him to one location and role, and Conan has to lose that position in order for a story to take form. However, closer study reveals that kingship is not only natural to Conan's character, but also that it reveals a nuanced understanding of the power of the sovereign. After all, Conan's very first story, "The Phoenix on the Sword," portrays Conan as king from beginning to end, so the character's kingship was clearly an integral part of how Howard viewed his character.

## The Sovereign and the *Homo Sacer*

Giorgio Agamben is an Italian philosopher strongly influenced by the writings of Foucault, Heidegger, and Benjamin. According to their theories, in the wake of the horrors of the concentration camps of the Second World War, our understanding of what constitutes sovereign power fundamentally altered. His writings since the 1990s have focused on the concept of the bare life, the human unprotected by law and thus exposed fully to sovereign power. He calls this figure *homo sacer*, a person who is not protected by the law and therefore can be killed by anyone. [338] According to Agamben, the power of a sovereign comes from the ability to turn a person into *homo sacer* by creating a "state of exception," which is to say, to make an exception to the law which protects life[339].

---

[336] Schweitzer, Darrell. "King Kull as a Prototype of Conan." *The Robert E. Howard Reader,* ed. Darrell Schweitzer. Rockville, MD: Borgo Press, 2010. 131.

[337] Schweitzer also refers to Conan climbing "the ladder of thief, pirate, soldier, military leader, and king." "Prototype"131-132. The idea of Conan climbing such a ladder from one position to the next is fallacious. It ignores the rises and falls in Conan's power, none of which seems to bother Conan much. For example, in "Black Colossus," a young Conan comes to lead the army of Khoraja, a position he leaves for unknown reasons to return to the life of a wanderer. The ladder idea also makes Conan seizing the crown seem the culmination of a preordained path rather than one event in a string of adventures. The nature of the telling of these stories, moving between times without apparent regard for a cohesive narrative, also seems to make an argument against viewing Conan's life as a rise in power leading towards the throne.

[338] Agamben, Giorgio. *Homo sacer.* Trans. David Heller-Roazen. Stanford, CA: Stanford UP, 1998. According to Agamben, the best example of *homo sacer* is a human in a concentration camp, someone who has been stripped of absolutely all else—rights, property, etc.—and is at the supreme mercy of the state. "From this perspective, the camp—as the pure, absolute, and impassable biopolitical space (insofar as it is founded solely on the state of exception)—will appear as the hidden paradigm of the political space of modernity." 72-73.

[339] "At once excluding bare life from and capturing it within the political order, the state of exception actually constituted, in its very separateness, the hidden foundation on which the entire political system rested." Agamben 12.

This state of exception is the suspension of the law, wherein the sovereign can suspend the protection the law gives his subjects. According to Agamben, it is the ability to lift the effect of the law which makes the law possible. A system exists because there must be those beyond its boundaries. [340] Agamben writes: "Inscribed as a presupposed exception in every rule that orders or forbids something (for example, in the rule that forbids homicide) is the pure and unsanctionable figure of the offense that, in the normal case, brings about the rule's own transgression (in the same example, the killing of a man not as natural violence but as sovereign violence in the state of exception)."[341] And, though Agamben probably did not mean it so literally, there can be no surer example of sovereign violence than a sovereign himself committing violence.

Agamben explains specifically the act of violence as the key to sovereign power. "…at its center lies a scandalous unification of the two essentially antithetical principles …, violence and justice. *Nomos* is the power that, 'with the strongest hand,' achieves the paradoxical union of these opposites."[342] Because the sovereign has the strongest hand, it has the power to do what would normally be a transgression of the law by suspending the law itself.

Conan perfectly illustrates his ability to create this state of exception to the law. Consider the scene in "The Scarlet Citadel" in which Conan stands atop the walls of Tamar, holding aloft Arpello, who attempted to usurp his power:

> "Take your plots to hell with you!" he roared, and like a sack of salt, he hurled the prince of Pellia far out, to fall through empty space for a hundred and fifty feet. The people gave back as the body came hurtling down, to smash on the marble pave, spattering blood and brains, and lie crushed in its splintered armor, like a mangled beetle.[343]

Conan, as king, has the power to make Arpello a *homo sacer*; not only that, but it is the power to kill Arpello, or anyone he chooses, without committing murder that makes him sovereign. This demonstrates his control over the law.

Another key moment that illustrates this appears in *The Hour of the Dragon*, in which Conan himself juxtaposes his sovereignty with his ability to do death. Even crippled by magic, Conan attempts to enforce his sovereign power by dealing death. He shouts, "I am the king! Death to you, dog-

---

[340] Which is to say, drawing the boundaries establishes not just what is outside but what is inside the border.
[341] Agamben 19.
[342] Agamben 24.
[343]*Coming of Conan* 110

brothers!" and looses an arrow at the enemy leader. [344] Had his arrow found its mark, the story would have gone very differently.

It is important to emphasize that the key to his sovereignty is not that Conan can kill without punishment. That would only make Conan a skillful murderer. Conan controls when the law that protects citizens from being killed is suspended. This violence is inherent not only to his kingship but to all sovereignty. As Agamben illustrates, "the sovereign is the point of indistinction between violence and law, the threshold on which violence passes over into law and law passes over into violence."[345]

## The Bandit and the Sovereign

In addition to being sovereign, Conan is also a bandit. These two identities are opposite in power but depend on each other for their existence. According to Agamben's theory, the bandit was the first form of the *homo sacer*, which in the modern period appears in the form of the concentration camp internee.[346] In the form more relevant to Conan, the *homo sacer* appears as a bandit. Agamben explains, "The medieval ban also presents analogous traits: the bandit could be killed." [347] The bandit is outside society but subject to its laws, hence why he can be killed with impunity. The sovereign—the king—is part of the society but not subject to sovereign power, as he himself wields it. It is the king who creates the bandit.

Cleverly, Agamben uses the word 'ban' to mean 'to make someone a bandit.' The ban is solely in the hands of the sovereign. The bandit and the sovereign are inherently tied together. Without a sovereign to establish a rule of law, the idea of a bandit would be meaningless, as there would be no legal system for the bandit to exist outside of. As Agamben writes, "The ban is the force of simultaneous attraction and repulsion that ties together the two poles of the sovereign exception: bare life and power, *homo sacer* and the sovereign."[348] "Bare life" is life that is not protected by the law, which has been stripped of all qualities save the fact of being alive. It does not have a voice, rights, or a role in the state. The bandit exists in a legal borderland--a "zone of indistinction"--as it is neither inside nor completely outside the state, neither a citizen nor a foreigner.

Both the king and the bandit exist in the state of exception. Just as the *homo sacer* stands outside a society's laws but is subject to the exercise of sovereign power, the king exists inside a society but is exempt from its laws,

---

[344] Howard, Robert E. *The Bloody Crown of Conan*. Ed. Patrice Louinet. New York: Ballantine Books, 2004. 102.

[345] Agamben 25.

[346] Agamben describes the camp as "the pure space of exception." 78.

[347] Agamben 63.

[348] Agamben 66.

able to carry out violence at will.[349] Each is connected to the other by the violence that makes both possible. Agamben explains, "Sovereign violence is in truth founded not on a pact but on the exclusive inclusion of bare life in the state. And just as sovereign power's first and immediate referent is, in this sense, the life that may be killed but not sacrificed, and that has its paradigm in *homo sacer,* so in the person of the sovereign, … dwells permanently in the city."[350] Agamben does not consider, though Howard clearly does, that sometimes that sovereign must leave the city when he needs to take killing those he bans into his own hands.

Thus, the sovereign exists in a zone of indistinction, both inside and outside a society. It is this existence which makes sovereign power possible:

> The paradox of sovereignty consists in the fact the sovereign is, at the same time, outside and inside the juridical order. If the sovereign is truly the one to whom the juridical order grants the power of proclaiming a state of exception and, therefore, of suspending the orders own validity, then the sovereign stands outside the juridical order and, nevertheless, belongs to it, since it is up to him to decide if the constitution is to be suspended *in toto.*[351]

We see this duality expressed in the form of Conan, who is explicitly bandit and sovereign in one. Even when he does not hold a legal title, his ability as the sovereign to kill without committing murder brings him great power. He exists beyond the law. Conan, as king or as bandit, is never subject to the law as a citizen with rights who is being tried. The single time we see Conan in a court, in "The Queen of the Black Coast," it is as witness to protect his friend--and Conan ends up killing the judge and cutting his way out of the court with his sword.[352]

The bandit, as Agamben explains, can also kill, because the bandit has what amounts to a constant death sentence. As the laws do not protect him, they do not constrain him. Agamben suggests that the bandit's power to resist violence is inherent to the sovereign's *ban,* the ability to make someone a bandit. One who is exposed to death can no longer be accused of committing a crime, so anything he or she does from that point on is neither legal nor illegal. As Agamben explains, "Corresponding to this particular status of the 'right of Punishing,' which takes the form of a survival of the state of nature at the very heart of the state, is the subjects' capacity not to disobey but to resist violence exercised on their own person, 'for … no man is supposed

---

[349] Agamben 17 quoting Carl Schmitt. "The specification that the sovereign is '*at the same time outside and inside the juridical order*' (emphasis added) is not insignificant: the sovereign, having the legal power to suspend the validity of the law, legally places himself outside the law. This means that the paradox can also be formulated this way: 'the law is outside itself.'"

[350] Agamben 64.

[351] Agamben 17.

[352] *Coming of Conan* 123.

bound, by Covenant, not to resist violence; and consequently it cannot be intended, that he gave any right to another to lay violent hands upon his person' ([Leviathan])."[353] Even the bandit can resist violence upon him: this is not a right, but a condition inherent in life, which fights for itself.

It is vital that Conan is very rarely seen in a position other than of a leader or a roving bandit who makes his own rules, which is to say he is always a sovereign and bandit. Even in the stories in which we do see Conan as a follower, he is never a true subject of a sovereign. In "The Pool of the Black One," Conan obeys the orders of Zaporavo only until the opportunity arises to fight and kill him. In "Black Colossus," the narrator reminds the reader that Conan is a mercenary and not a regular soldier. To reinforce this point, Amalrus, the captain of the mercenaries, separates Conan even from his comrades: "That's Conan the northron, the most turbulent of all my rogues! I'd have hanged him long ago, were he not the best swordsman that ever donned hauberk—"[354] The narrative insists that Conan is a bandit at heart, even when he follows orders, which he clearly chafes at having to do at all. He may do as he is told for a time, but he never becomes a citizen, subject to the sovereign power. He is never protected by a state's laws.

Death threatens not only the bandit, however. Agamben goes on to discuss that the killing of the sovereign, like the killing of the bandit, cannot be considered murder. The sovereign, like the bandit, can be "killed but not sacrificed": "for the sovereign, death reveals the excess that seems to be as such inherent in supreme power, as if supreme power were, in the last analysis, nothing other than the capacity to constitute oneself and others as life that may be killed but not sacrificed."[355] This killing, while a political crime against the state, would not be murder. Agamben explains the sacrifice in this context as a killing within the juridical order, a legally sanctioned execution that does not intrude on the continuity of sovereign power. We certainly see this being the case with Conan.

Even when he is king, Conan's life is constantly in danger, and those who seek to kill him can expect no resistance except that which he can deal himself, by his own power. Thus, Conan, like all sovereigns, has something of the bandit in himself. As a bandit, when his bare life is subject to violence, he protects himself to the full extent of his ability. From this position, we see Conan's slaying of the former king Numedides as a clear illustration of the zone of indistinction between sovereign and bandit. In a fight to the death for the kingship, both parties simultaneously create the state of exception and experience its effects: each may kill the other, and whoever kills the other will have done so while making the other a bandit. We see this played out when the passing of sovereign power, in the image of the crown, is shown as a

---

[353] Agamben 64.
[354] *Coming of Conan* 167.
[355] Agamben 61.

direct result of this act of violence. In Conan's own words, "King Numedides lay dead at my feet and I tore the crown from his gory head and set it on my own."[356]

The conflicts in the Conan stories challenge not only Conan's statesmanship but also the might of his sword-arm. As such, Conan embodies the zone of indistinction between sovereign and bandit, between the law and nature. He does not move from one identity to the other, but is both at once.

## Conan and the Social Contract

As Agamben's theories illustrate, Conan's own perspective on his kingship is decidedly modern. Conan dismisses contemporary theories about the state as "outworn lies," and the stories clearly undermine the theory of the social contract supported by John Locke and the early statesmen of the United States, demonstrating instead a system of power based on the ability to do violence. In Conan's strong right hand is ample proof that his power comes not from the consent of those he governs but from his own capacity to place others into the legal "zone of indistinction" that allows him to kill them without committing murder, thus doing as he pleases.

Though it would have been impossible for Howard, who died in 1936, to access the ideas of Giorgio Agamben, who was born in 1942, Agamben based some of his theory on Hobbes's *Leviathan*. Agamben used Hobbes's work's explanation of the creation and function of a single powerful sovereign power. According to Hobbes, humans in the state of nature commit violence unrestrainedly, and it is the function of the state to restrict that. For the state to function, one member must nevertheless continue to exercise the power to kill: the sovereign himself. In this text, Agamben sees the figure of the sovereign who controls the right to violence, alone among people to maintain the power to kill which existed in the state of nature: "Sovereignty thus presents itself as an incorporation of the state of nature in society, or, if one prefers, as a state of indistinction between nature and culture, between violence and law, and this very indistinction constitutes specifically sovereign violence."[357] Conan, who enters the kingship as a barbarian existing in a state of nature, is perhaps the perfect embodiment of this idea.

Conan specifically figures himself as a barbarian king, declaring his right to rule based on his martial prowess rather than by divine right. When Conan faces down the pretender Amalrus in "The Scarlet Citadel," the latter's plot to replace Conan on the throne of Aquilonia has been revealed. Conan, his army crushed and his body weakened by poison, still defies Amalrus, comparing his own claim to sovereignty with that of Amalrus:

---

[356] *Coming of Conan* 11.
[357] Agamben 27.

> Your fathers did the fighting and the suffering, and handed their crowns to
> you on golden platters. What you inherited without lifting a finger – except
> to poison a few brothers – I fought for. You sit on satin and guzzle wine
> the people sweat for, and talk of divine rights of sovereignty – bah! I climbed
> out of the abyss of naked barbarism to the throne and in that climb I spilt
> my blood as freely as I have spilt that of others.[358]

Here we see Conan distinctly separating himself from those who claim a
divine right to rule, challenging the established notion of kingship. Instead,
Conan presents himself in a very modern framework, which anticipates the
political changes Agamben perceives in the twentieth century. Conan is both
one who can create a state of exception in putting others to death, as a
sovereign, and also one who can have his blood freely spilled, as a bandit.

Drawing on Hobbes's idea of the violence wielded by the sovereign,
Agamben argues that power comes not from the consent of the governed
but from the exercise of power, which originates in the sovereign itself, not
in those who are subject to it.[359] It is clear in the Conan stories that Conan's
right to rule does not come from a social contract. A quote from *The Road of
Kings*, quoted in *The Scarlet Citadel*, explicitly sets Conan's violence against
another theory of sovereignty, the divine right to rule: "Gleaming shell of an
outworn lie; fable of Right divine—/You gained your crowns by heritage,
but Blood was the price of mine."[360] Agamben would remind us that, in truth,
this is the only source of sovereign power, and that "outworn lie" only ever
masked the truth.

Though Conan wishes to rule in the best interest of the people, he
frequently is pitted against them. In Howard's stories, the will of the
populace, represented by the mob, is frequently an enemy of Conan, turned
against him by demagogues. While Conan rules in *The Phoenix on the Sword*, a
poet called Rinaldo encourages the mob against him. "He idealizes the king
whom Conan killed to get the crown, remembering only that he occasionally
patronized the arts, and forgetting the evils of his reign, and he is making the
people forget."[361] Faced with a discontented populace, Conan has to turn to
his weapons and ability to kill at will: the source of his sovereign power.

Conan fears there is something more sinister behind these murmurs and

---

[358] *Coming of Conan* 91.

[359] "Contrary to our modern habit of representing the political realm in terms of citizens'
rights, free will, and social contracts, from the point of view of sovereignty only bare life is
authentically political. This is why in Hobbes, the foundation of sovereign power is to be
sought not in the subjects' free renunciation of their natural right but in the sovereigns
preservation of his natural right to do anything to anyone, which now appears as the right to
punish." Agamben 64.

[360] *Coming of Conan* 122.

[361] *Coming of Conan* 9.

exclaims, "If I could but come to grips with something tangible, that I could cleave with my sword," to which his retainer Prospero replies, "Let the people snarl! The mercenaries are ours, and the Black Dragons, and every rogue in Poitain swears by you."[362] Prospero expresses his belief that the military power behind Conan is stronger than that opposed to him, but Conan's wisdom goes deeper. When his reign and life are threatened, he asks, "Who dies first?"[363] As king, he is not subject to the law, and therefore can kill as he pleases--he can make any enemy of his *homo sacer*. Conan places foremost in his thinking the ability to do death with impunity to those who oppose his sovereignty. This suits perfectly his role as bandit-sovereign, who exemplifies both forms of indistinction.

## Conan as King

It is his dual identity that makes Conan not only a powerful ruler but a good one. Despite what the reader might expect from Conan's barbarous ancestry and bloody rise to power, he presents himself as a benevolent ruler. By embodying both sides of the zone of indistinction, Conan forms a political whole.

When Conan confronts Tarascus after the final battle in *The Hour of the Dragon*, he invites him to come face him and pit his strength against his. Conan, who is still king, says, "Why do you stand afar off, dog of Belverus? I can't reach you; come in and die!" Indeed, Conan seems to relish making them both subjects of bare life, each vulnerable to being killed without punishment. By doing so, he recreates the zone of indistinction that existed when he killed Numidides. This raw state beyond the juridical order is natural for a barbarian, but is also key to being sovereign.

And finally, Conan demonstrates his ability to control the zone of indistinction between violence and the law in another way when he offers to spare his enemy's life, a life the law would condemn. Conan demands of Tarascus at the end of the novel:

'Do you yield?'
'Will you give me quarter?' demanded the Nemedian.
'Aye. Better than you'd have given me, you dog. Life for you and all your men who throw down their arms. Though I ought to split your head for an infernal thief,' the Cimmerian added.'[364]

The "ought" shows that he knows the law, but Conan is not bound by his own statutes, and therefore exercises pure sovereign power over his subjects.

---

362 *Coming of Conan* 12.
363 *Coming of Conan* 29.
364 *Bloody Crown*. 253.

This power is limited only by his own mortality. In other words, taken from the opposite perspective, Conan's power is only as strong as his ability to hold it. This is why, as a barbarian, he is perhaps the perfect king for his world: one whose immense strength keeps his grip firmly on his sovereignty, and not plots, magic, or demons can take that from his grasp. He is a king because he is also a "man" (in, of course, Howardian terms). Because he is a barbarian, he is perfectly suited to living in the state of exception. This is why he can so adeptly wear the crown. He does not need to fear the power of the juridical system—he wields it in his right hand.

# CONCLUSION: THE PROBLEMATIC LEGACY OF THE WEIRD TALE

The natural function of the weird subgenre is to subvert readers' expectations. This is most familiar in the stories presenting a world that is, on the surface, consistent with the reader's familiar world, but reveals forces that urbanized readers dismiss as impossible to be lurking just below the surface. Weird fiction suggests these invisible forces—cosmic horrors, black magic, and half-forgotten unhuman beings—are ready to burst into the open or be discovered by those who suspect their existence. It is perhaps even more interesting, however, to search for other ways this subversion functions: by guiding readers into looking below the surface of accepted ideologies and revealing marginalized, repressed, and silenced statuses that usually function invisibly and go unquestioned. Thus, the weird tale is in a unique position as a site of ideological friction and subversion.

In many cases, the text itself challenges conventions, either explicitly or implicitly. For example, Lovecraft's "The Unnamable" challenges the contemporary construction of aesthetics and literary authority, representing the superiority of weird writers over the literary mainstream. Other texts, while seemingly upholding accepted norms, provide a way to challenge and problematize them by exposing implicit assumptions about hierarchies of ideas. In this and other celebrations of the "weird class," as I have termed it, we find the establishment of a separate class based, in part, on its sensitivity to understanding the world in terms the majority cannot imagine.

I cannot finish this book without a discussion of another cultural conflict that shapes this fiction. Racist, misogynistic, and otherwise hateful content often appears in weird fiction in general and *Weird Tales* in particular. Much has been written about whether the opinions of Lovecraft, Howard, and others reflect that they were products of their time or demonstrates a choice by those who were exposed to inclusive ideas. Following these critiques, I seek to examine how these writers reproduced, occasionally challenged, and reinforced ideologies of race and gender. While it can be said that both writers did question, to varying degrees, these views, it must also be acknowledged that often the anxiety that they employed in their writing came from a personal fear of seeing those norms subverted, such as Lovecraft's fear of losing the privilege his whiteness brought him. I cannot describe these depictions without condemning them, and I also feel I should do so thoroughly, in order to illustrate how these texts not only repeat ideological constructions of race but also how they themselves shape those same ideologies by weaving them into the system of values suggested by their narratives. Perhaps in this they can serve as a tool for understanding the complex ideological role of literature.

To illustrate this point, as I have described in Lovecraft's "The Horror at Red Hook," Lovecraft's personal disgust at the multicultural population of his New York neighborhood influenced his creation of a story that explicitly connects non-Anglo characters with diabolical acts and breeding with nonhumans. In this and other texts, Lovecraft reified ideas about the moral and cultural superiority of whites, particularly those descended from English families. Not only in Lovecraft but in many *Weird Tales* stories, characters meant to be more sympathetic to the reader are described as more white, while the Otherness of antagonists is often presented as synonymous with their reprehensibility and corruption.

While there are somewhat sympathetic portrayals of nonwhites in Howard's works and in other weird fiction written in his time, even then they often mirror contemporary racial imagination which implicitly valued whiteness over all other racial identities. Thus, a close reading of these texts provides a complex picture in which racist ideology is subverted in some ways and reinforced in others.

One of the clearest illustrations of this is that sympathetic nonwhite characters are stressed as having physical features that are close to those of whites. Their behavior, likewise, is described as adhering to the white ideal. In Howard's "The Spirit of Tom Molyneux,"[365] the black boxer Ace Jessel is described as "tall, clean-limbed and rangy, long and smooth of muscle, clear of eye and broad of forehead."[366] Jessel's value is established through the eyes of the white narrator, value that the narrator insists is in spite of his race: "I knew the real nobility underlying Ace's black skin."[367] In short, the qualities in Jessel the narrator most admires are the ones he considers to be the most white. To emphasize the difference between the black boxer and his white manager, Jessel speaks in a minstrel-show version of black dialect: "Ah ain't nevah met no man yet what could even knock me off mah feet, but Ah reckon dat nigguh can."[368] Thus, the qualities the narrator judges as virtues in the black character are either white values or markers of Otherness.

In direct contrast to Jessel, his opponent, Mankiller Gomez, is described in overt terms of his African origin, which is depicted in animalistic and inhuman terms that draws on depictions of black men as apes: "His soul was abysmal. He was ape-like, primordial—the very spirit of that morass of barbarism from which mankind has so tortuously climbed, and toward which

---

[365] This story was published in the April 1929 issue of *Ghost Stories*.
[366] Robert E. Howard, *The Horror Stories of Robert E. Howard,* New York: Ballantine Books, 2008, 71.
[367] Ibid., 69.
[368] Ibid., 69.

men look with so much suspicion"[369] It is of particular note in this description that it is assumed that the gaze of "men," a category that does not include Gomez, categorizes Gomez below humanity itself, according to the hierarchy in which the white "race" is the most evolved and thus farthest from its animal origins. His physical description emphasizes his difference not only from Ace but from humanity: "His small bullet head was set squarely between gigantic shoulders, and his forehead was so low that his kinky wool seemed to lower over his small bestial and bloodshot eyes."[370] A similar description can be found in Howard's "Black Hound of Death," in which the description of a black antagonist is not only a mirror of the one from "The Spirit of Tom Molyneux" but focuses even more on inhuman, gorilla-like features:

> He was like a shape from the abyss whence mankind crawled ages ago. His primitive ferocity was reflected in the bulging knots of muscles that corded his long, massive apish arms, his huge sloping shoulders; above all the bullet-shaped head .... The wide, flat nostrils, murky eyes, thick lips that writhed back from tusk-like teeth—all proclaimed the man's kinship with the primordial.[371]

It can be said that there are aspects of this story that problematize the question of race, but they do not remove the racist beliefs of a racial hierarchy that shape the story. While a "White Hope" is sought to defeat the champion Gomez, in the end it is Ace Jessel who must fight him to win, subverting the premise that a white man must be found to defeat the black champion. On the other hand, Jessel is childishly deferential to his white manager, thereby reaffirming the racial hierarchy in all but physical prowess—and the idea of the superiority of black people in strength in itself echoes antebellum arguments for the naturalness of the slaveholding system.

In another challenge to racial conceptions, Jessel is aided by the ghost of this black boxing champion, Tom Molyneux, who has the "killer instinct" Jessel lacks and guides Jessel's fists to strike true. In this, perhaps, can be read the heroic idea that a true champion is a fighter whose greatness extends past his era and his death so that he can help others of his race, the same way Kull travels forward through time to help the Pictish king Bran Mak Morn win a battle in the Howard story "Kings of the Night."[372] Bran, it is revealed, is descended from Kull's friend Brule the Spear Slayer. Even this connection, however, serves to reemphasize racial divisions, further emphasizing the distinctness of different "races" and underlining racial essentialism. Kull

---

[369] Ibid., 68.

[370] Ibid., 71

[371] Robert E. Howard, "Black Hound of Death," *Weird Tales*, November 1936, 420-421.

[372] Robert E. Howard, *Bran Mak Morn: The Last King*, New York: Ballantine Books, 2005, 31.

could travel in time because of this blood link. This links characters to "their own" race, races that are essentially separate, with qualities that are inherent and unique, further underlining the fear of racial mixing that pervades much weird fiction of this era.

Thus, even when it is challenging some contemporary hegemonic beliefs, the weird tale may affirm others, basing its attack on separations of identity that reveal a deep-seated bias that the reexamination of hierarchy does not shake. In this, it does not differ from stories of any period, which reproduce contemporary ideologies. A given story questions certain ideologies, but the ones it does not must also be held up to the light. Examining these texts reveals how deeply-rooted ideologies can be affirmed even when they are challenged, thus making the challenge itself a tool of perpetuating Othering practices. The texts delineate which beliefs are open to question and which are not, even to the point that they are not even mentioned as anything but natural.

In closing this discussion, I feel it is important to mention that not a single writer of color has been found in the pages of the Edwin Baird or Farnsworth Wright eras of *Weird Tales*, from the inception of the magazine in 1923 to 1940.

The role of weird fiction in upholding despicable ideologies is one troubling aspect of it that all scholars of the subject must contend with, and it is important to use it to understand and illustrate how such ideological practices function while simultaneously condemning their content. I hope I have succeeded in doing that. There are other ways this book is limited. The length of this collection does mean that it has certain limitations. In focusing on the Lovecraft Circle, I have both neglected the broader sphere of the *Weird Tales* writers and restricted my examination to the first half of the 20th century. As such, I have not looked at later or contemporary weird fiction and the way it has continued to develop and shift. This would make for a work at least as long and rich as the current, not to mention would allow for a study of how themes that were problematic in texts from that era are now addressed.

This work has also focused on the writers of the Lovecraft Circle and their influences. A more complete examination of weird fiction would look at other writers and traditions of this subgenre, such as the popular work of Seabury Quinn, whose Jules de Grandin stories were most frequently chosen as the best stories of *Weird Tales*. A closer examination of female writers of weird fiction would also be vital to understanding the function of weird literature in terms of gender. Despite the humble scope of this work, I hope it will encourage and support further research into weird literature and the many art forms it has influenced.

## Bibliography


Moore, C. L. *Shambleau and Others.* New York: Gnome Press, Inc. 1953.

Moore, C. L. The Best of C. L. Moore. Ed. Lester del Rey. New York: Nelson Doubleday, 1975.

Howard, Robert E. "Black Hound of Death." *Weird Tales*, November 1936.

Howard, Robert E. *Bran Mak Morn: The Last King.* New York: Ballantine Books, 2005.

Howard, Robert E. *The Horror Stories of Robert E. Howard.* New York: Ballantine Books, 2008.